Goals, Goals, Goals

THE POSH DIARY 2010/11

Compiled by Paul Donnelly & Paul Mitchell

GOALS, GOALS, GOALS : THE POSH DIARY 2010/11

ISBN : 978-095631-103-0

First Published 2011 by
WHIRE DRAGON PUBLISHING
Peterborough, England.

Cover photograph by kind permission of www.theposh.com
and Joe Dent

Back cover photographs by kind permission of
Peter Berridge & Steve Turner

Cover design by Chris Slade

Once again thank you to everyone who has taken the time to contribute to the book – it was a great effort from all the contributors to get their reports done so quickly and at such short notice.

Thank you to Bob Symms and the media staff at PUFC for their help and we are delighted that they have contributed to the book. Thank you also to Darragh MacAnthony for giving us his enthusiastic backing.

Many thanks to Chris Wilkinson of uptheposh.com for the stats and John Verrall of posh.footballblog.co.uk for allowing us to use some of his match reports.

As always thank you to the community at londonroad.net for their enthusiasm and support.

And to my girls Roma and Bella. They still don't ask me what the score was but they were glad I had a nice day out at Old Trafford.

Paul Mitchell

This book could nor have happened without the generous assistance of countless individuals who share their special Posh moments from the 2010/11 season.

To all of you, I extend my deep appreciation.

KIP & FTC

Paul Donnelly

Foreword

My Grandad took me to my first Posh game back in the days of John Cozens, Chris Turner and Eric Steele. My memories from that night are sketchy, but I do remember Cozens scored a belter. I remember seeing the delight on my Grandad's face as the whole ground celebrated. I also remember my Dad holding my brother and I back in the London Rd tunnel as Notts Forest fans 'visited' the London Rd faithful just after a League Cup tie.

I remember the original 'Argentina' kit, I remember Greig Shepherd, Gary Worrall, Bryn Gunn, Jimmy Holmes and of course dear old Bill Harvey. I remember Glebe Rd in all it's open glory and I remember the feeling of seeing my team run out to The Post Horn Gallop. I have seen some wonderful performances and I also saw some absolute dross. But if the players wore 'Upon this Rock' on their chest, then it was my job to cheer them on through rain, shine or snow and I was only too pleased to do so.

These memories and more make me very proud to say that my daughter Gemma is now a confirmed fourth generation Poshie. Sorry Gem. I emigrated to Texas in 2002. Since then, my Posh viewing has been limited to three games per year.

Match days are different for an ex-pat. A lot of it will depend on where we are in the world. For me, in Texas, 3pm games kick off at 9am….7.45pm games kick off at 1.45pm. So I wake up Saturday morning, and by 11am my weekend is either made perfect by a win…or ruined by a defeat. No trips to Ebeneezer's, no away game road trips and no time for any real pre-match anticipation.

Ex-pats use every available method to get news of the game. T.V, internet, phone calls and the Radio Scum phone-in to listen to Bob from Rings End, so he can tell us all about how Joe Lewis would be better off being played as a winger and

CMS should be in goal . We will use any method that gives us a better understanding of how the boys in blue are performing.

Supporting Posh from afar over the years has brought a full range of emotions, just as I am sure it has for those that attend every week. But those emotions are different. Of course we are always delighted when we win….but also devastated at not being able to enjoy the victory. We are pissed off when we lose, but thankful that we haven't had to endure the frustration of a poor performance, or a crap referee.

I wasn't able to make one game this past season, so I'm not sure I'm really qualified to write anything for this book. But I was fortunate enough to be able to witness the games live on Sky via the internet and the Play-Off Final was live on TV. For me, this season was all about getting back in the Championship and although we took a heart-stopping route we achieved our goal.

I love what Darragh MacAnthony has done for Peterborough United. I love that he has turned us from a laughing stock into a well-respected ambitious club. I love that he has been able to restore pride in the team throughout the city.

So….. how was it to be 5000 miles away from the action this season? One word sums it up…. tough. Tough to go through all the management comings and goings. Tough not to be able to witness the class of CMS, the silky skills of Boyd, the set pieces of McCann and the battle of Zakuani. Tough to hear the goals go in (both ends) and only picture them in my mind. Tough not being able to breakdown each game with friends But toughest of all is simply not being able to watch my team play.

Supporting Posh is so much more than cheering on our local team…it is born into us, bred into us and royal blue runs from us when we bleed.

From the first game my Grandad took me to until the last game I witness, no matter where in the world I am I will always be PROUD TO BE POSH.

Nigel Curtis

Introduction

When I first came back to the club, I had worked out that 17 victories would get us promoted automatically. We knew that it would be a tough ask, but I also had belief in the players that they could achieve what was set out for them.

The run that we went on, where we won seven out of eight matches, made me confident that we could achieve automatic promotion, but the late goals we conceded against Bournemouth at London Road and then at Huddersfield killed us and to be fair I knew after the draw at Huddersfield that we wouldn't make the top two. Southampton were on an excellent run and credit to them for that.

The night before I was appointed, I watched from the stands as we beat Brentford and I knew straight away that the system had to be changed because Grant McCann couldn't operate in a two- man midfield, I needed to utilise this valuable asset.

I knew that we had enough good players to operate with the diamond system and we worked on it ahead of the Brighton game, but the most worrying aspect of that performance was the lack of self-belief that the players had, which was strange because when I was here before, the mentality was one of the key reasons behind our success.

The lads were lacking confidence for whatever reason and we had to install some new belief straight away and ensure that the players went into every game believing they could win. After the Huddersfield game, we knew we would be in the play-offs and I really wanted to play Milton Keynes Dons because I felt that the system we used would suit us down to the ground.

Unfortunately in the first-leg we didn't keep the ball well enough and if I am honest, I may have picked the wrong team, but when Mark Little went on that run and Grant stuck away that penalty, I felt that we would get promoted. Our preparation for the second-leg was spot on and tactically we got it right, the lads went out there and delivered a great performance, we ran all over them and could have, and should have, won by more.

For the final itself, I was really relaxed. I think semi-finals tend to be more tense and that actually stemmed from the fact that I believed we would win the final. I knew it would be hard, but the size of the pitch and the confidence that the players had would give us a great chance of winning if we turned up and we did just that.

The players take the credit, my staff and the team behind the scenes have worked extremely hard and now everybody can look forward to the new season in the Championship.

Darren Ferguson

August 2010

07/08/10

Peterborough United 3 - 0 Bristol Rovers

Boyd '57
Mclean '73
McCann '88

Posh: *Lewis, Little, Langmead, Wesolowski (sub Lee 76min), Mclean (sub Tomlin 78min), Boyd, McCann, Mackail-Smith, Bennett, Mendez-Laing (sub Davies 60min), Nana. Unused subs: Rowe, Piergianni, Koranteng, Collis.*
Bristol Rovers: *Anderson, Sawyer, Coles, Tunnicliffe, Campbell, Hoskins, Hughes (sub Lines 72min), Anthony, Blizzard, Brown (sub Duffy 83min), Kuffour. Unused subs: Regan, Green, Richards, Reece, Shallow.*
Attendance: *7,133 (661 Rovers fans)*

OK. So it's probably fair to say that 2009/10 wasn't the best of seasons. We struggled at the start of the season and when Fergie left in murky circumstances we were doomed.

Despite having an obvious talent for watching videos, Mark Cooper was palpably out of his depth. Fortunately, he had the bumbling Exodus to shield him from the worst of the fans' ire. Gannon improved things a little, but was cuckolded into staying in Stockport. He split opinion amongst the fans, but for me anybody who drops CMS in favour of Reuben Reid is a little mushy upstairs, to say the least.

And so to Johnson. If anything, we were worse in final throes of 2010 under (lest we not forget) the former C*mbridge boss. But that didn't matter, he was a proven manager, with success at Yeovil and Bristol City. There were posts on Londonroad.net from Bristol City fans, forewarning of dubious tactics and strange, nepotistic signings – mostly dismissed at the time.

The summer went well in terms of signings - we'd even

heard of Grant McCann. The others: Dave Hibbert, Kelvin Langemead, James Wesolowski, Nathaniel Mendez-Laing and Seth Nana Ofori-Twumasi all sounded reasonably promising - or frightening if you're Bob Burrows - they were joined by Davies, Collis, the now permanent Little and not-very-footballer-looking Lee Tomlin. This seemed to address, if not completely solve, the problem areas from the relegation season.

Pre-season was, as ever, an irrelevance and largely ignored – by me at least – and so it was with some excitement that I pitched up at London Road on 7 August. Pre-match predictions were wild, but the general consensus was positive – we should have too much for Rovers, particularly with the returning Boyd ready to link up with Mackail-Smith and Mclean.

We started badly, but that was OK, these things can take time. Lewis made a couple of magnificent saves as Rovers stepped up the pressure before half-time. Langemead looked ponderous and was lucky to stay on, Wesolowski looked lost and McCann was generous with our possession. Worst of all, Mclean had failed to gather all of his toys up from his summer dummy-spit and looked disinterested.

As the ref blew-up, my thoughts turned towards the bottom of the table rather than the top. The summer signings were expensive and I was already starting to wonder how long Darragh's patience would last. Then my thoughts turned to a bottle of Coke.

Whatever Johnson said to the players at half-time clearly worked. A different team came out for the second half and following a brilliant, persistent, stumbling run from Langemead they were fortified by an early Boyd goal. I've no idea what Nottingham Forest did to George, but their loss was already our gain.

Mclean got a second after a fine pass from Boyd, making up for a clutch of missed chances and with CMS at his effervescent best, the Trinity were back. As the half went on, Posh turned on the style, with McCann controlling the game from a little patch of grass just inside our half.

Tomlin came on and looked a right nasty little shit. Within a couple of minutes he'd run his studs down a couple of Rovers players' calves and hit a rasping shot just over. McCann put Rovers out of their misery, finishing things off direct from a free kick and Johnson entertained the LRE at the end of the game with a Fryesque running fist-pump. Hmmmm.

The first game of the season is always a difficult one to judge. You have no idea if you have just beaten the champions or the worst team ever. Even during the game, Posh were frustratingly inconsistent. Terrible, clumsy and slow in the first half – electric in the second.

You start a season full of questions and hope to have some of them answered by the end of the first game – in this case we were left with more questions than answers. Perhaps it is best left to Johnson to sum up, with the intelligence that came to personify his time in charge: *"There's a long way to go yet but you couldn't have wrote a book about a better start."*

Stuart Lee

* * * * *

10/08/10

Peterborough United 4 - 1 Rotherham

Bennett '34	Marshall '9
Boyd '39	
Mclean '60	
Mackail-Smith '85	

Posh: *Lewis, Little, Langmead, Lee, Wesolowski, Mclean (sub Tomlin 70min), Boyd, Mackail-Smith, Bennett, Mendez-Laing (sub Hibbert 67min), Nana (sub Rowe 67min). Unused subs: Piergianni, Koranteng, Davies, Collis.*
Rotherham: *Warrington, Newey, Harrison, Cresswell, Law, Taylor (sub Warne 75min), Le. Fondre, Brogan, Ashworth, Ellison, Marshall. Unused subs: Green, Banks, Darley, Annerson.*
Attendance: *4,145 (242 Rotherham fans)*

August 2010

Wembley bound once again, this time in the League Cup or the Carling Cup as we should refer to it nowadays. Better than the Milk Cup admittedly and at least as a product it's more healthy for you.

Yeah, we despatched the might of Rotherham, the mighty Millers from oop' north. Yet somehow we managed to go one behind as early as the ninth minute, whilst it wasn't one of Joe's biggest clangers, I am sure he'd hold his hands up and admit he could've done better - sadly an all too often used phrase over his Posh career. Though he wasn't helped by a failed clearance by NML who otherwise did OK.

The highlight of the game was the fact that the Holy Trinity were on fire and proved too much for the opposition. As someone shouted at one of their defenders who looked harassed and really wishing he was somewhere, anywhere else "Don't worry mate, they've embarrassed better than you over the years"

Unfortunately Aaron received what, at the time, looked a nasty injury. He is one of the few professional footballers who only goes down when genuinely injured so there were was some concern.

A typically poor gate for a League Cup fixture - even though the club made an effort making some tickets cheaper - but to be honest the competition really doesn't have any attraction until the later stages. It was overall a good professional performance and is ever the case in cups, it is the result that matters.

Ann Thrax

* * * * *

13/08/10

Rene 'Is he still bloody here?' Howe joins non-league Rushden & Diamonds on a loan deal until the beginning of January.

* * * * *

14/08/10

Bournemouth 5 - 1 Peterborough United

Pugh '10 — Langmead '61
Robinson '20
Pitman '50, '57, '65

Bournemouth: Jalal, Pearce, Bartley, Wiggins, Cooper, Pugh (sub Cummings 86min), Robinson, Purches, Symes (sub McQuiod 78min), Pitman. Feeney (sub Arter 85min) Unused subs: Stockley, Bradbury, Garry, Thomas.
Posh: Lewis, Nana (sub Rowe 46min), Little, Langmead, Bennett (sub Hibbert 68min), Wesolowski, McCann, Boyd, Mendez-Laing (sub Lee 46min), Mackail-Smith, Mclean. Unused subs: Collis, Piergianni, Davies, Tomlin.
Attendance: 5,949 (760 away).

Despite 26 years supporting Posh, and my previous match having been the 6-0 thumping at Reading, I went to this match filled with confidence that I was travelling down to the South coast to see Posh pick up three points against newly-promoted Bournemouth. We'd started the season brightly, scoring seven goals in dispatching Bristol Rovers in the opening league match and Rotherham in the League Cup, and having kept the majority of the players who'd got us out of League 1 the last time. All was pointing to a comfortable win. A decent trip down on the train, followed by a couple of beers and lunch with my Bournemouth-resident sister, had further lightened the mood.

What a difference 90 minutes makes. Scrap that – what a difference 20 minutes makes. 20 minutes in, we were 2-0 down, and it was clear that another weekend away was going to be ruined by a miserable afternoon at the football. Full backs Nana and Little had been taking it in turns to allow Bournemouth's wide players through, the Posh midfield was chasing shadows, and the whole side looked sluggish and lethargic. Posh fans were in good voice though, and somehow the team made it through to half time without conceding any more.

This was the first time I'd seen summer signings Nana and Mendez-Laing, and they'd both been dreadful. Fortunately, Gary Johnson seemed to recognise as much, and took them both off, replacing them with Charlie Lee and Tommy Rowe.

Things were looking up now, surely? Apparently not. Five minutes into the second-half, it was all over, as Pitman scored his first to give Bournemouth a 3-0 lead. Posh fans were now pretty subdued, with a handful at the back singing supposedly amusing songs about the food they'd eaten, and how bad Posh were. My sense of humour not quite being in tune with theirs, it only served to further piss me off.

Pitman's second goal, Bournemouth's fourth, came shortly afterwards, with Lee proving no more able than Nana to deal with Bournemouth's wide players. Posh finally got one back, with Langmead bundling a corner past the impressive former Posh bench warmer Shwan Jalal. Even I couldn't summon up much optimism that the comeback was on though. On 65 minutes, Pitman completed his hat trick with a curling shot past Lewis. Johnson reacted to the fifth goal with the Fry-esque tactic of chucking on another striker, with Dave Hibbert coming on for Ryan Bennett. Surprisingly enough, it didn't work, and the match finished 5-1.

A poor performance, and a terrible result. All made a little weirder by cryptic (and never explained) comments from Gary Johnson that the team's below par performance was caused by "circumstances" which he couldn't talk about, but which would all come out one day. Conspiracy theories abounded, from players being hungover or suffering from food poisoning , to a player having a crisis in his personal life, to gamesmanship on Bournemouth's part, overwatering the pitch before the match and at half time – plus many more.

My take on it? We were just rubbish.

James Wilson

* * * * *

21/08/10

Peterborough United 4 - 2 Huddersfield Town

Peterborough United	Huddersfield Town
Boyd '45	Rhodes '22
Mclean '50, '67	Carey '33
Mackail-Smith '52	

Posh: *Lewis, Little, Langmead, Wesolowski (sub Lee 84min), Mclean (sub Hibbert 81min), Boyd, Mackail-Smith, McCann, Bennett, Davies, Nana (sub Rowe 46min). Unused subs: Piergianni, Mendez-Laing, Collis, Tomlin.*
Huddersfield: *Smithies, Peltier, Gudjonsson, Clarke, Garner, Pilkington (sub Croft 69min), Johnson, Arfield, Rhodes (sub Novak 65min), McCombe, Carey (sub Roberts 61min). Unused subs: Kay, Robinson, Bennett, Ridhalgh.*
Attendance: *6,647 (1,064 away)*

Who would have thought that this would be the first of four matches to be contested between two of the more fancied teams in the division?

The first two home games of the season had resulted in two wins with a 7-1 aggregate score. After sweltering, and getting soundly thrashed, in the first away game at Bournemouth the previous Saturday - and with all sort of excuses being put forward by the management for that display - we went into this game hoping that the Bournemouth result had genuinely been caused by some 'mysterious stomach bug.'

I invited a couple of friends along for the match and convinced them that they would definitely see goals, as our first three matches had yielded a total of 14. They also happened to be Kettering Town supporters and I considered it my duty to try to convert them to proper football.

Within half an hour we were 2-0 down and my friends had disappeared. However, we managed to get back into the match, and just before half time Boyd scored a rather soft goal, with the help of 'Udder's keeper Smithies, but what the hell?

The second half saw the 'MacAttack' at its very best, two from Aaron and the other from the League's future top scorer. Posh had managed to keep their home record intact and it was a thoroughly good game, played at a superb tempo and no little skill - and this was despite fielding Nana for half the match, and Langmead and Davies for the whole match. Six goals, five yellow cards and only one point away from the top. What a game and what a start to the season!

The two friends who left just before half time had gone for a pint in The Peacock, missing all four of the Posh goals. They had watched the scores coming in on the TV and were pretty pissed at leaving too early. To be fair I have managed to drag both of them along a couple of times since, Craig even managing to get to the Old Trafford Final.

Dave Allen

* * * * *

24/08/10

Peterborough United 2 - 1 Cardiff City

Mackail-Smith '74 Bothroyd '33
Boyd '88

Posh: *Lewis, Rowe, Nana, Langmead, Bennett, Wesolowski, McCann, Boyd, Davies (sub Lee 89min), Mclean, Mackail-Smith. Unused subs: Collis, Zakuani, Hibbert, Piergianni, Mendez-Laing, Tomlin.*
Cardiff: *Heaton, Naylor (sub Quinn 88min), Hudson, Whittingham, Bothroyd, Burke, Gerrard, Koumas, Olofinjana (sub McPhail 33min, sub Wildig 82min), Drinkwater, Matthews. Unused subs: Marshall, Gyepes, Taiwo, Jarvis.*
Attendance: *3,806 (299 Cardiff fans)*

Posh fixtures against Cardiff have a history of producing classic moments. A 3-0 win on the way to promotion in 1991, the highlight of which being an invasion of City fans dressed as Arabs chasing Paul Culpin as he was on his way to scoring, was the first time I saw the two teams play. 2003 saw a tiny crowd on a Tuesday night with big spending Cardiff vying for promotion and Posh scrambling for survival, a great performance saw us win 2-0 and the entire crowd clapping along to the Great Escape. Finally, Posh fans will never forget the game last season as Posh managed to come back from four goals down at half-time to equalise in the final minute of the game.

So, when it came to the game this year it seemed an easy decision to make to head down to London Road to watch the second round of the Carling Cup. However, this game was up against the opening night of the Beer Festival and I already knew of a few Posh fans who had decided that real ale took priority over the football. Those who did so looked like they had made a good decision at half time. Posh had played poorly and Cardiff had dominated possession from start to finish. Fortunately, we only let one goal in, leaving the game still in the balance.

The second half was better but still Posh couldn't score. That is, until the 74th minute when CMS scored an absolute belter at the London Road end of the ground to ignite hopes that we could have another memorable match on our hands. Lo and behold in the 88th minute Posh did it, and it was one of the players who had scored in the 4-4 game that scored the winner. Another Boydie classic gave the goalkeeper no chance and saw Posh to victory. Another chapter in the Posh v Cardiff saga was complete.

Daniel Ferguson-Thomas

* * * * *

28/08/10

Plymouth 0 - 3 Peterborough United

Mackail-Smith '61, '75
Mclean '77

Plymouth: *Button, Duguid, N'Gala, Johnson, Clark, Patterson, Bhasera, Mason (sub Maclean 71min), Noone, Molyneux (sub*

Patterson 88min), Parrett (sub Peterlin 75min). Unused subs: Larrieu, Summerfield, Timar, Nelson.
Posh: *Lewis, Nana, Rowe, Langmead, Bennett, Wesolowski, McCann, Boyd (sub Tomlin 79min), Davies (sub Mendez-Laing 56min), Mclean (sub Hibbert 79min), Mackail-Smith. Unused subs: Zakuani, Lee, Piergianni, Collis.*
Attendance: *7,712 (274 Posh fans)*

As is normal on a match day, muggins was awake, way before the alarm had even had a chance to realise I was asleep. What is it with my body clock that goes totally haywire before a football match that I'm attending.

Plans for the day had been made and I was expecting a friend who would be staying over to make sure he didn't have to worry about a five hour journey back north after a long drive down to Bristol plus a train ride, drinks, and a footy match...It's a "fair old poke" to Plymouth.

Paul arrived at about 7.30 and after a coffee we set off for Avonmouth and the 8.04 to Temple Meads, giving us plenty of time for a hearty breakfast at our first Wetherspoon of the day, The Knight's Templar, tucked neatly away behind Brunel's majestic station. With breakfast consumed it was back to the station to board the 09 17 for Plymouth and the pre-arranged tour-de-wetherspoon that I had planned.

After leaving the train it was up hill to an area of Plymouth called Mutley Plain and a pint at The Mannamead - no other Poshies about but it is a bit off the radar of the normal Posh supporter. However, I digress, having asked instructions on the quickest way to get to The Gog and Magog, there was a convenient bus stop outside, but not at journeys end it was another monumental walk across a big square and down a couple of side streets. Is it possible that Plymouth is the only city in UK with signposts to the local red light district. There were signs everywhere to "The Plymouth Ho" and I thought that was just an American term.

Anyway having met a couple of fellow supporters, it was down pint and off to The Union Rooms, I was assured it was only a couple of hundred yards, just felt more like a couple of miles.

Four down one to go, I thought, but having discussed the alternatives we decided to taxi it to The Britannia where we hoped to bump into a few more friendly faces. The pub by this time was heaving to the rafters with both sets of supporters. I met so many people I recognised it would be unfair to name names and disappoint those who's names I forgot to mention. We eventually decided it was worth leaving the pub - having travelled this far it would be rude not to attend the match Posh took to the field wearing the previous seasons away strip of sky-blue and white stripes, matching my attire, so I knew that if there was an injury scare Gary Johnson could always call on me.

0-0 at half time and I was beginning to wish I'd stayed in The Britannia. However, several Posh supporters at half time were more optimistic than me and placed their spare change on Posh to win 3-0 at 20/1. Why did I not do the same? Idiot. As history and the record books will show they were right to be so confident. The Mac Attack supplied all three goals.

At full time we walked rapidly back down the hill to the railway station and jumped on the first available train to Bristol. Sadly, upon said train must have been the only guard in the UK who actually checks the tickets presented to them. Mine was for the next train, so he said I would either have to get off at Exeter or pay the extra. I said we'd get off at Exeter and about two hundred yards from the station is, guess what, a Wetherspoon called The Imperial. We had about an hour to waste so we sat outside and managed to find a couple of disgruntled Plymouth supporters who had made the journey from Barnstaple and weren't best pleased with the result.

Discretion being the better part of valour we decided to leave early for the train. Trouble is there is not a direct bus service back to mine from Temple Meads which meant changing somewhere, so I suggested changing at the top of Park Street right outside, you guessed it again, The Berkeley. We had twenty minutes to spare and it would have been rude not to go in.

Later, on leaving the bus, the pavement decided to wobble and come up and meet me at a rate of knots - I still have the scar.

Nick Prince

* * * * *

September 2010

04/09/10

Tranmere 1 - 0 Peterborough United

Mendy '44

Tranmere: *Collister, Cresswell, Goodison, Blanchard, McGurk (sub Brown 67min), Grandison, Darville, Mendey, Showunmi, Thomas-Moore, Fraughan. Unused subs: Cathalina, Wood, Power, Coughlin, Bakayogo, Akins.*
Posh: *Lewis, Whelpdale, Langmead, Bennett, Rowe, Davies (sub Hibbert 24min), Wesolowski, Lee (sub Tomlin 56min), Boyd, Mclean (sub McCann 70min), Mackail-Smith. Unused subs: Collis, Zakuani, Piergianni, Davies.*
Attendance *4,636 (312 away)*

Before the match Tranmere boss Les Parry said that "I want to be a team that's horrible to play against". He succeeds, as Tranmere grabbed a surprise first win of the season.

Adam McGurk forces Joe Lewis into a save in the opening minutes; a poor backpass from Chris Whelpdale, returning from injury, gifts McGurk a second chance, but he pulls his shot across goal. Liam Darville denies Aaron Mclean a shot, before Aaron Davies is forced off with a muscle injury. Posh continue to have chances, but Charlie Lee puts his shot over, while Ryan Bennett and George Boyd are denied by the crossbar and home keeper Joe Collister in quick succession.

The hosts take the lead just before the break as a mistake by Lee lets in McGurk, who gives debutant Arnaud Mendy a tap in. In the second half Posh are unable to hit the target: first Dave Hibbert then James Wesolowski fire wide. Grant McCann is sent on despite having played for Northern Ireland in Slovenia the night before, and immediately sends a 30-yard free kick inches over the bar. Posh continue to have chances, but the home side hold on for the three points and a clean sheet.

Chris Wilkinson

* * * * *

11/09/10

Peterborough United 5 - 2 Oldham

Wesolowski '45	Jones '19
Mclean '62	Taylor '38
Boyd '71	
Hibbert '82	
McCann '90	

Posh: *Lewis, Langmead, Bennett (sub Zakuani 46min), Rowe, Whelpdale, Tomlin (sub Mendez-Laing 68min), Boyd, McCann, Wesolowski, Mackail-Smith, Mclean (sub Hibbert 81min). Unused subs: Lee, Piergianni, Collis, Davies.*
Oldham: *Brill, Hazel, Jones, Jarrett, Furman, Feeney, Taylor, Lee, Stephens (sub Kelly 85min), Black (sub Smalley 78min, Tounkare. Unused subs: M'Voto, Jacobson, Kelly, Grega, Dikaba, Gerrard.*
Attendance: *6,337 (381 Oldham fans)*

At the beginning of last season I was one of those who fully believed our momentum from the previous two campaigns would to lead us to another challenge for promotion. I do tend to go a little over the top, and this time around expected us to be struggling to stay in League One. Bringing in a manager that I'd actually heard of; players such as Grant McCann; and the brilliant news that Boydy had signed a new contract made me fully believe that we could be making a very quick return to the Championship.

My match day routine barely changes throughout the season. As a member of the PISA committee I plan to arrive at Ebeneezer's on Grove Street (good food, cheap beer, and good company) for midday so that I can do my usual match day duties, and as usual I roll out of bed at midday, make noises about getting the bus into town until my girlfriend gives me a lift to Eb's.

Pre-match we're still moaning about the abysmal 5-1 defeat at Bournemouth but I try to convince everyone that they'll be there or there abouts at the end of the season so a defeat away at Bournmouth perhaps isn't the end of the world. What does look to be certain is that Sheffield Wednesday, who currently lead the table, will be making an immediate return to the Championship. Today's opponents Oldham are one of several team just a point behind Wednesday so most in Eb's are predicting a closely fought contest.

After five years at University in Sheffield I finally have my first ever season ticket at London Road and stand half way back slightly to the left of the London Road End with various other regulars. No matter who the game is against it's usually the same lot and it hasn't taken long to figure out whom not to share my opinions on Langmead with.

Twenty minutes in and Posh are a goal down, we're looking brilliant going forward, but Oldham look dangerous with every attack. Still, a point against one of the title contenders would still be a good point. Five minutes to go until half-time, and Oldham make it 2-0 with another good cross, this time from the other side. Can't see us getting back into this one now......then Wes pulls one back to make it 2-1 at the break. It's an odd feeling going into half-time losing, but happy that we're only a goal down. We've fallen behind in our previous three home games and then gone on to win, so on the whole the general feeling is one of optimism.

Posh started the second-half well, but needed a spark to get things going. Ritchie Jones kindly provided that spark for us when he decided to contest a dropball, what followed is what I believe is known as a 'melee'. Three yellow cards later Posh resumed play with a long thrown-in which Aaron heads in, 2-2. Ten minutes later the place goes wild as Boyd put us into the lead.

Posh were not easing off. Ritchie Jones was staring into the LRE with disbelief at what had just happened, in return the LRE were offering their opinions of him in the usual fashion. Jones had completely forgotten that he was supposed to be defending a corner, and almost fell on his arse as Hibbert made it 4-2. For the second time his season we'd come from 2-0 down to make it 4-2. Deep into injury time McCann managed to go one better. 5-2, and top of the league on goals scored.

What a game.

Nick Warrick

* * * * *

18/09/10

Exeter City 2 - 2 Peterborough United

Nardiello '54 — Archibald-Henville (og) '29
Cureton '71 — Tomlin '82

Exeter: *Jones, Tully, Duffy, Dunne, Archibald-Henville, Harley, Nardiello (sub Cureton 65min), Golborne, Jones, Sercombe, O'Flynn (sub Logan 58min). Unused subs: Krysiak, Noble, Cozic, Edwards, Thomson.*
Posh: *Lewis, Langmead, Zakuani, Rowe, Whelpdale, Wesolowski (sub Nana 38min), McCann (sub Hibbert 75min), Boyd, Mendez-Laing (sub Tomlin 70min), Mclean, Mackail-Smith. Unused subs: Collis, Lee, Piergianni, Davies.*
Attendance: *5,146 (319 Posh fans)*

St James Park is a ground I've never managed to tick off the list, I've gone past it many times on trips to Torquay and Plymouth, and so this took a little bit of planning…

So, Saturday 18th September 2010. Well actually the story starts a little earlier than that. Nearly ten months and three months earlier to be precise, let me explain. For those that know me well don't need telling, it had something to do with my love of wine. Christmas 2009 Stef and I received a voucher from her two kids, Lee and Jade, for a wine tasting experience (there draws to a close a quick chapter one).

Chapter two begins in mid-June as the fixtures for the 2010/2011 season are announced and I start to plan those free weekends when Stef doesn't have the children. Now back to the voucher. There was a choice of six locations across the UK stretching from Cambridge to Shropshire and from Kent to Devon. Having spent a Sunday afternoon researching the web we had it narrowed down to one in Kent and one in Devon.

It just so happened that we had both booked Friday 17 September off work due to an annual event, which as things transpired we were not going to attend. I suggested we use this day off - remember the fixtures were out at this point – and did the romantic thing and suggested we take the Thursday off work, travel down to Bishopsteignton in Devon have a night in a hotel followed by wine tasting the next day. Well Bishopsteignton is a reasonably small place so it transpired the best idea was to book the Southgate hotel in Exeter for the three nights and catch a train to the vineyard, we wouldn't have to drive and could enjoy a nice weekend away. Stef was delighted which was when I said, to my amazement, that Posh were believe it or not playing Exeter on the Saturday.

Chapter three, wine tasting over on the Friday, we made our way back to the hotel and were in the hotel bar when a fleet of taxis turned up and out popped around 20 large strapping rugby chaps from Newcastle Falcons, much to Stef's delight. Half an hour later up draws a Florida coach and off gets the Posh team, coaches and management team.

Having grabbed a light dinner we popped back down to the bar and I introduced myself to Gary Johnson, politely explained that the weekend had already cost me enough and asked him to ensure that we came away with three points. A couple of drinks followed including buying Mr Fry a large red wine - which to my disgust and the barman's amazement he takes with ice.

Chapter Four, we were joined on the Saturday morning by my brother Mark and his partner, Natalie, who had booked themselves into a city centre Exeter hotel for the Saturday. Having commenced another one of the legendary Venters drinking sessions before the game we took a little walk (or stagger) through Exeter's equivalent of Millfield and found ourselves, the only Posh fans, in a little pub close to the ground.

As this was Natalie's first Posh away game the discussion soon moved on to the search of ladies handbags by stewards on the way into the ground, and sure enough as we entered she was asked by a female steward to open her handbag - she promises on her next away trip she'll put something in there to make it worth the search.

We made our way into the St James Terrace open away end, which was as narrow as narrow can be, with a view that was certainly not the best. The game itself was very entertaining as was the discussion with a poor unfortunate next to me who was adamant that Wesolowski crossed the ball that caused the panic for an own goal putting us 1-0 up (by the way I was right it was NML who crossed, and it's fair to say there is some difference between the two players, and not only in their height). This was a fairly comfortable game we thought at half time, backed up just after the break when CMS hit the bar. I thought that was a good time to toddle off to the gents. On my way out of the gents, I was stopped by a sprightly old lady complaining bitterly about the ladies toilet which was nothing more than a shed. At that exact moment an Exeter forward, I forget his name, nor do I care, scored and both of our reactions were - 'here we go again'.

Shortly afterwards they scored again and the weekend was taking a turn for the worse. But then the lad who makes me feel it's ok to be a little plump, Lee Tomlin, popped up and brought us back level.

The final chapter of the game was back and forth and somehow (and probably the only decent thing he ever did for us, apart from leaving for the Cobblers) Nana scrambled away a shot off our line with virtually the last kick of the game.

We left the ground, and spent the evening enjoying a few more drinks in Exeter city centre, polished off too much food, and decided it was best ahead of the drive home to head off for an early night. It was either that or Mark had decided the stewards were right to search Natalie's bag and there was something in there to make their evening go with a buzz.

Paul Venters

* * * * *

21/09/10

Peterborough United 1 - 3 Swansea City

Mackail-Smith '7 Sinclair '5, '41, '78

Posh: *Lewis, Nana (sub Jay Davies 86min), Langmead, Zakuani, Rowe, Whelpdale (sub Tomlin 56min), Mendez-Laing (sub Hibbert 70min), Lee, Boyd, Mclean, Mackail-Smith. Unused subs: Collis,, Piergianni, Davies, Ralph.*

Swansea: *Malambay, Williams, Tate, Cotterill, Pratley, Van Der Gun (sub Allen 70min), Dobbie, Lopez (sub Gower 68min), Serran, Sinclair (sub Dyer 81min), Richards. Unused subs: Orlandi, Cornell, Donnelly, Alfei.*

Attendance: *4,164 (188 Swansea fans)*

Kids for a fiver anywhere night, not a Gary Glitter special but a promotional Posh push to get more through the gate. Youngest child was away on a school residential trip, so I took the older lad down to London Road as there was nothing on the telly. Feeling like a change of scenery we sat on the original 1913 wooden seats in the main stand, sacrificing comfort for the sake of historical accuracy.

We were optimistic before this one kicked off, we'd matched Swansea 2-2 in the Championship the previous season, and I once saw them get mullered 8-0 by Liverpool in an FA Cup replay, so we sat back to watch the goals flow in. To add to the excitement, just before kick-off the well tanned, finely honed yet slightly bloated figure of a man glided past us mere mortals on his way to the press box, attracting glances from fans up and down the stand. "Who IS that?" asked my son. "That my boy is Alan Swann. He's a bit of a dibdob".

Swansea had Scott Sinclair in their ranks and he tore us to bits within five minutes Sinclair beat my Nana every which way before smacking the ball into Lewis and rebounding it in for the opener. We were back level within a minute thanks to CMS hammering in a long range five yard effort. The Welsh referee decided that one goal was plenty enough for us as he then failed to see a blatant penalty as CMS was hauled down in the box. Cue screams of outrage from the London Road End, and mildly irate tutting from the main stand faithful. Meanwhile, Sinclair continued to tease and taunt my Nana, twisting him inside and out for the remainder of the half, and leaving him for dead again just before half time before blasting home his second of the night.

Second half went much the way of the first, another blatant penalty waved away by the Welsh ref, my Nana in bits as Sinclair went on to claim the match ball by finishing from a sweet backheeled layoff from somebody in white (wasn't paying attention by this time). CMS managed to sky over the bar from two yards out - it was that kind of night. To think, he finished his Posh career on 99 goals as well.

Swansea went on to bigger and better things, and are gracing the Premiership next season. Posh went on to bigger and better things, and will be gracing the Championship next season.

Dick Ard, Thrapston

* * * * *

25/09/10

Peterborough United 2 - 1 MK Dons

Mackail-Smith '36 Lewington '37
Mclean '48

Posh: *Lewis, Langmead, Zakuani, Rowe (sub Little 76min), Whelpdale, Gill (sub Lee 79min), McCann, Boyd, Tomlin (sub Mendez-Laing 89min), Mclean, Mackail-Smith. Unused subs: Collis, Hibbert, Davies, Nana.*
MK Dons: *Martin, Lewington, Doumbe, Mackenzie (sub Chicken 85min), Easter, Guy, Woodards, Hammann (sub Wilbraham 66min), Ibehre, Leven, Chadwick. Unused subs: Searle, Carrington, G. Baldock, Howell, Flanagan.*
Attendance: *7,838 (818 Dons fans)*

God I f**king hate the imposters I really do. Not because of any fictitious rivalry we are meant to have with them on geographical grounds or even any on the pitch threat they may offer us. No, I, like most football fans, hate them because of how they got into the league. The Football League should hang their heads in shame for ever and a day for allowing it to happen.

Anyway we beat the bastards today with a not totally convincing performance admittedly but enough to do them good and proper. CMS put us one up after putting away a one-on-one with consummate ease and then a bit of a cock-up resulted in Lewington, the ginger whinger, scoring an equalizer. I have to admit he is one player I'd have fancied seeing play for us, although he would have to dye his hair and stop being the arse he normally is.

The team were not exactly warmly applauded off the pitch but neither were they booed off which perhaps shows a little bit of maturity amongst us moany Posh fans. Gary Johnson does not seem to be the sort of manager I thought he would be, he is not at all animated on the touchline and seems to think merely wearing a Posh scarf shows his commitment. However, he seemed to have said something at half-tme as the team came out looking much more like we would expect.

Aaron scored our second goal and for a fair bit of the game we looked in control although we had a nervy last ten minutes. To be honest, I think the nerves were more from the fans than on the pitch and Zac in particular was immense: one particular amazing, and for him typical, last ditch challenge stood out. Even Langmead, dare I say, looked ok which for him should have been enough to retire there and then as he'll probably never reach such dizzy heights again.

Along with most of the near 8,000 crowd went home happy and who gives a shit about those that didn't as they don't support a proper football club anyway.

Paul Donnelly

* * * * *

28/09/10

Peterborough United 2 - 3 Notts County

Zakuani '36 — Davies '31, 34'
Mackail-Smith '59 — Westcarr '43

Posh: *Lewis, Langmead, Zakuani, Whelpdale, McCann, Rowe, Gill, Tomlin, Mclean, Boyd, Mackail-Smith. Subs: Little, Hibbert, Mendez-Laing, Collis, Davies, Lee, Ofori-Twumasi*
Swansea: *Burch, Thompson, Pearce, Harley, Edwards, Davies, Ravenhill, Westcarr, Bishop, Judge, Smith. Subs: Rodgers, Nelson, Jervis, Spicer, Chilvers, Hawley, Hubbins*
Attendance: *6,136 (675 Notts County fans)*

At the start of the season I attempt to plan my business and private diary around the fixture list so I was a tad piffed off when the Works Director on a contract we had in Harrogate, North Yorkshire decided to bring forward the deadline on the handover of three flats.

When these guys say "jump" I reply with "how high" after all they put food on table etc. I crossed out Notts at home in the diary, gave my season ticket to a mate and after an eventful three hour journey in Gregorz Ford Transit we arrived on site the Monday before the game.

Halfway through the Tuesday Mowlsey rings me: "what time you in Ebz tonight, I've taken your advice and been out and smartened myself up"

"I'm up in North Yorks mate, will have to give it a miss"

"F★★★kin pretend Posh", was his reply

Ummmmmm, had he been to Niro's? Had he been to Next? Had he been to George@Asda? Had he been to Lidl or had he simply found a bag of clothes outside someones house destined for a charity in Zingywali when we all know they end up at a car boot sale in Wisbech.

F★★K it,

"Gregorz can I borrow your van?"

"Yeah no problem, you going up the shop?"

"Yeah see you guys downstairs for breakfast at 7-30am Wednesday"

I left Harrogate at 3.30pm and did OK until I hit Donny, slow traffic until nearly Newark as a series of lorry's decided to bring the A1 down to 56mph as they jockeyed for position.

Pull into the carpark at 6.30, bag of chips and curry sauce - half of which I dropped down my T-shirt - and into Eb's for a pint of London Pride, feeling proud that unless Chris Dowsett travelled up from Pompey I could be only Posh fan in the ground that had travelled 160 miles to support his team.

Then I clocks Mowlsey: blue polo shirt, chino cargo shorts and boat shoes, the same clobber he's worn the previous 328 times I'd seen him

"Where's ya new clobber then?"

"Here," he said, pointing down to some new leather laces

Off to the match, shit I had no season ticket, 20 bleedin' quid, up the tunnel of love, banged the left hand side of the tunnel three times and the right twice (it's a good luck thing) and joined the swaying 15,000 on the LRE kop.

Birthday boy Gary Johnson had named an unchanged side for

the visit of Notts County. The visitors score first when Big Joe let Davies poke one through his legs. Davies's second was a belter and the travelling 600 odd Magpies were jubilant. Zak got one back for us, then they went 3-1 and all this before half time. Some one who runs a lot up front for Posh scored in the second to make it 3-2.

FULL TIME, then DING, DING, DING seconds out round one. Scuffles, red cards for petulance, pitch invasions and even the odd streaker. As long as it's occasional and no one gets hurt it all adds a bit of colour. However, what was described as a mass brawl in the media was no more than a lot of shoving though from our LRE ringside advantage point we could clearly see Tomlin relishing the opportunity to deliver a couple of stunning kidney shots, while Richardson waded in as if someone had just stolen his Lev Yashin keeper gloves. The kids chanted "fight fight fight" and the Stewards did a superb job one in particular who jumped the wall to land a right hander on the Notts no 5.

1am: back in my Harrogate Stink Pit, £100 lighter and nil points…that's Posh for you.

Paul Donnelly, Whittlesey

* * * * *

October 2010

02/10/2010

Carlisle United 0 - 1 Peterborough United
Mackail-Smith '32

Carlisle: *Collin, Simek, McDaid, Murphy, Robson (sub Norwood 46min), Taiwo, Zoko, Marshall (sub Curran 46min), Madine, Berrett (sub Price 86min), Chester. Unused subs: Hurst, Kane, Caig, McKenna.*
Posh: *Lewis, Langmead, Zakuani, Rowe (sub Nana 46min), Little, Davies, Gill (sub Lee 78min), Boyd, Tomlin, Mackail-Smith, Mclean (sub Frecklington 87min). Unused subs: Collis, Hibbert, Whelpdale, Mendez-Laing.*
Attendance: *5,735(296 away)*

Personally, one of the very few positives to come out of the dismal 2009-2010 relegation season was that Posh would be pitting their wits against Carlisle; the only club in the Football League that doesn't involve me jumping through hoops and/or spending a small fortune to get to (I live in Glasgow). Naturally, when the fixtures list was published, Carlisle United away was the first fixture that I zoned in on. I was pretty happy with the outcome; fairly early in the Season and not at a time of year where I would have to spend two hours wearing several layers of clothing.

The day itself started rather farcically. I had managed to rope in my longsuffering mate, Izzy (who couldn't be less interested in football), on the promise of beer and some food. Unfortunately we had been at a friend's birthday do the night before and both of us overslept, missing our train to Carlisle. After having dashed to Central Station feeling a little peaky, a sympathetic Fat Controller took pity on us and allowed us on the relatively plush Virgin train, rather than the wino express which we were due to get.

A short while later we rolled into Carlisle. The town itself is, frankly, one of the oddest places I have ever been to (and I have been to a few). Most of the inhabitants seemed to have a few chromosomes missing, and, being a border town, the whole place was decked out like something from an EDL rally. It also seems to be stuck in some kind of time warp, as demonstrated by the pet shop selling cats in cages of twenty and the newsagents with the Spastic's Society charity box outside.

We slowly sauntered through town towards a pub that had been recommended on a well known unofficial fans forum. The pub was The Howard Arms and was very pleasant; good beer, friendly staff and a nice garden. We had a few drinks and watched whatever Premier League game was on that day (I think it involved Wigan) in the company of a handful of good-natured Carlisle fans. The only downer was the food - my cheese pie was unintentionally mature and Izzy's fish smelt of cat food. However, at a couple of quid each, one can't really complain.

At around half-two, we headed to the aesthetically-odd but rather quaint Brunton Park. I had underestimated how long it would take us to get there, so our relaxed amble quickly turned into that awkward mince one does when you need to get somewhere quickly but are too embarrassed to run. (A word of warning: a combination of fatness, unfitness, beer and mouldy pie can lead to a stitch of monumental proportions). Unfortunately, the away terrace was closed, so the Posh fans were huddled into a small section on the end of the new(ish) all-seater stand (at £27 per ticket, London Road seemed like a bargain). We made our way to our seats just as the teams were coming out for the kick-off. Considering the distance, there were a decent number of Posh fans there, and I spied a few familiar faces, along with the much maligned G(S)CE lot.

Personally, the game was bookmarked by a number of 'hellos' and 'goodbyes'. It was my first 'in the flesh' of the cosmic Gary Johnson era, so it was my first opportunity to witness the stellar talents of names that would go down in Posh folklore, such as Kelvin Langmead, Aaron Davies and Nana Ofori-Twumasi. Little did I know at the time, but this would also be the last time that I saw Aaron Mclean pull on a Posh shirt.

The game itself was a rather forgettable affair. Craig Mackail-Smith and the portly Lee Tomlin shone, but the rest were distinctly average. Posh dominated for the first half hour and took the lead through a CMS one-on-one, the like of which Posh fans would become accustomed to over the course of the season.

However, after that it all went a bit rubbish. Defensively, Posh were very suspect; Langmead struggled, and future Premier League star Joe Lewis fumbled a number of chances onto the plates of the Carlisle players. Fortunately, the Carlisle team had the finishing ability of eleven Andrew Fotiadis's, so Posh somehow managed to scrape through with a clean sheet; one of only three achieved in Johnson's unremarkable tenure. Cue mass relief amongst the Posh following, chants of "wanker, wanker" from the GC(S)Es and Johnson doing that silly air-punch thing that he likes to do. I left pleased with the result (even Izzy enjoyed herself), if a bit worried about our prospects of promotion.

After leaving the ground, we headed back to the station, grabbed a quick pint and then waited for the train back up to Glasgow. We didn't miss that one.

Patrick McDevitt, Glasgow

* * * * *

05/10/10

Huddersfield Town 3 - 1 Peterboro' United 2

Carey '6 — Mclean '51

Pilkington '12, '24 — Little '87

Huddersfield: *Bennett, Peltier, Gudjonsson, P. Clarke, Kay, Pilkington, Johnson, Lee (sub Rhodes 66min), Novak, Ridehalgh, Carey (sub Crofty 71min). Unused subs: Allinson, Garner, N. Clarke.*
Posh: *Lewis, Nana, Langmead, Zakuani (sub Davies 46min), Little, Boyd, Lee, Frecklington, Mendez-Laing (sub Tomlin 46min), Mackail-Smith, Hibbert (sub Mclean 46min). Unused subs: Collis, Gill.*
Attendance: *2,904 (179 Posh fans)*

The day didn't start until 2pm for me, I got bladdered the night before and forgot to turn up to my Uni lecture (students, eh?) so when I did stir from my pit, I got ready and met my Leeds - and part time Posh - supporting mate in Leeds City Centre for some pre-match beers.

We took the short trip from Leeds to Huddersfield at about 5pm, had a few pints in Huddersfield city centre before stumbling over to the Galpharm for a rather rubbish competition sponsored by some paint company.

The guy behind the bar quizzed me about our team. I, being rather confident, and for some stupid reason placing faith in GJ to pick a decent team, told him we'd 'beat them by two or three' and 'only use 'second gear'. He laughed at me as he gave me the drinks and probably short-changed me too.

A Posh fan I know goes to Uni in Huddersfield, so I invited him to join me and the Leeds fan for drinks. The Leeds fan was curious about our team, he knew the stars, Boyd, Mclean, Mackail-Smith, Lewis etc from our time together in League One but was very intrigued about the new lot. I bigged up Tomlin and Little and slated Nana. We walked over to the Galpharm, and ended up paying to get in the home end due to very poorly signposted turnstiles. Luckily, a steward spotted the Posh shirts and took us to the away end before we got to our seats.

The game, well, I looked at the team out on the pitch, and saw Hibbert playing which was something rarely seen, Mendez-Laing and Nana were also playing plus an appearance by Zakuani which I was delighted about.

It didn't take long for things to turn bad as Carey hit an effort from about 25 yards and Joe had one of his infamous moments. He got down well, but somehow managed to let it smash him on the arm and roll in to the net. Awful error and we were 1-0 down after about five minutes. Huddersfield then decided to turn on the style, and Pilkington vs Nana was quite possibly the most one sided battle I have ever seen on a football pitch. Nana can't cope with a 90 year old with no legs, nevermind a player of Pilkington's quality. Nana was constantly on his arse, or being beaten with a simple bit of skill. Hudds clocked this very quickly and everything was being fed out to Pilkington.

Twelve minutes in, and Pilkington had enough of toying with us and decided to smash one in to the corner of the net with a sublime effort after cutting inside the quite awful Nana. Joe had no chance with this one, and 25 minutes in, Pilkington did it again, but this time, instead of toying with just Nana, he decided to torment Langmead and Charlie Lee as well and curled another beauty past a helpless Joe.

It was getting embarrassing, and I felt like I'd wasted money coming from Leeds, nevermind the hundreds around me who had travelled from Peterborough. We rarely tested the palms of ex Poshie Bennett. The only people looking like changing that were Boyd and CMS. Mendez-Laing and Frecklington were hideously disappointing. Charlie Lee burst forward and hit the bar with the only real chance Posh had before half-time.

At half-time, I made a dash to get one of the worst pies I've ever eaten - cold was an understatement, and it definitely wasn't meat inside - and take a quick slash before going back for another 45 minutes of torture. Luckily, Johnson noticed he had got it horribly wrong and hauled off Zakuani, Mendez-Laing and Hibbert and stuck on Lee Tomlin, Aaron Mclean &

Arron Davies. Charlie Lee switched to center back whilst Davies slotted into midfield.

Tomlin immediately had something to do; playing through Craig Mackail-Smith but the tireless front man put it just past the post. Then, suddenly, we were celebrating a goal. A cross from Nana - probably the only decent contribution he made in this match, and his Posh career - was headed in by Aaron Mclean. Game on.

After a brief spell of Huddersfield pressure, to remind us they were still alert; Posh started to play well, and really got going. Frecklington was still wasteful with possession but Posh were now pushing Huddersfield hard, and the hosts were wobbling.

Late in the second half, with about five minutes left, we were right back in it. Arron Davies sent in a cross and right back Mark Little headed in from all of about four yards with a diving header. No idea why he was there, no idea how he got there but he was and that was all that mattered. Unfortunately, we couldn't find the equaliser to take it to penalties, and went out, but the second half had given me a lot of encouragement. My Leeds supporting mate and I went back to the pub, he complimented CMS, Boyd, Mclean and Tomlin but hammered Langmead, Frecklington, Lewis and Nana. I couldn't really argue, the first four were brilliant; the latter four were beyond poor.

We jumped on a train to Leeds and enjoyed a few more pints discussing the game, rather interestingly he said: "I can't see Johnson lasting the season if you keep playing like that." I laughed at him and said: "Darragh won't sack him, he's learnt from last season".

Conor King

* * * * *

09/10/10

Hartlepool United 2 - 0 Peterborough United

Hartley '44
Liddle '90

Hartlepool: *Kean, Austin, Collins, Hartley, Horwood, Liddle, Gamble, Murray (sub Haslam 69min), McSweeney (sub Bjornsson 87min), Larkin (sub Behan 64min), Monkhouse. Unused subs: Devlin, Boyd, Yantorno, Fredriksen.*
Posh: *Lewis, Little, Langmead, Zakuani, Mclean, Boyd, Mackail-Smith, Davies (sub Mendez-Laing 89min), Nana (sub Bennett 85min), Tomlin, Gill (sub Frecklington 60min). Unused subs: Collis, Lee, Piergianni, Whelpdale.*
Attendance: *3,047 (381 Posh fans)*

Before I start I just want to point out that this game was my absolute low point of the season. People might be wondering why when defeat here left us in third place and only three points behind the leaders Brighton. This 90 minutes convinced me that a team under Johnson would not be getting promotion.

The day started as a usual away day from Chatteris does. Constantly checking my phone to see how many people would drop out just minutes before we left. Surprisingly the texts never arrived and at 9.15 I pulled up outside Dillon's house quickly followed by Pearsy's. Had a few laughs at Pearsy's ration bag for the day ahead. No matter what away game we go to he always brings a carrier bag with some life essentials in: a tube of Pringles, a bottle of water, todays paper and toilet roll. Now we were on our way and straight up a clear A1.

As we hit Hartlepool I should have sensed how the day was going to go. It was dull, windy and drizzling. Having spent a few years in the North I don't know why I was surprised. Stopped off in a well known fast food establishment and here my two passengers handed over their petrol money. As I was busy stuffing my face I put the money on the tray. Thinking nothing of it, I finished my meal, walked to the bin and tipped the contents into it. Still, thinking nothing of it I walked towards the door before my brain finally kicked in and I remembered. How all the teen mums and obese children laughed as I scrambled through the rubbish for my money.

We got lost in Hartlepool, which annoyed me. We then had to meet up with other people, which annoyed me. We wandered around for ages looking for a pub, which annoyed me. Then we didn't find a pub, which annoyed me. You can see how this day was going. Thankfully the woman in the ticket office couldn't read the expiry date on my Student Card and let me in on the cheap.

I can't really remember much of the game and I wont attempt to give a detailed match report. I seem to remember the game passing us by with no creativity and weak defending for their two goals. Late on Tomlin committed a needless foul leading to a three game ban topped it off.

Thankfully, the saviour returned and I guess I have now ticked off Hartlepool and I'll never have to go there again!

Chris Slade

* * * * *

16/10/2010

Peterborough United 5 - 4 Swindon Town

Mackail-Smith '3, '5	Ball '24, '43
Frecklington '22	Ritchie '30
Boyd '58	Austin '73 (pen)
Amankwaah (og) '90	

***Posh:** Lewis, Little, Langmead, Rowe, Zakuani (sub Lee 51min), Frecklington (sub Nana 70min), McCann, Boyd, Davies (sub Mendez-Laing 78min), Mclean, Mackail-Smith. Unused subs: Collis, Hibbert, Piergianni, Gill.*

***Swindon:** Lucas (sub Smith 46min), Cuthbert, Rose, Douglas (sub Prutton 70min), McGovern, Ferry, Pericard (sub Austin 29min), Morrison, Amankwaah, Ball, Ritchie. Unused subs: Caddis, O'Brien, Sheehan, Thompson.*

***Attendance:** 7,077 (494 Swindon fans)*

The great entertainers, goals galore at London Road, rampant attacking play and at least two home fans who left the ground absolutely fuming. This was school playground football at it's very worst and was in the eyes of the Standing On The Glebe (SOTG) hosts a clear sign that Johnson had lost the plot.

It was a pretty non-descript day, nothing out of the ordinary until the match started. We raced into a two goal lead thanks to the genius that is CMS, he even scored a one-on-one with the keeper, which at that stage of the season was still a relative rarity. Then, something happened that should have told the 7,077 people in the ground that it was going to be a strange old day....Lee Frecklington not only passed the ball forward, he scored with a pretty tidy finish. So, 3-0 up after 22 minutes and all is well with the world. Now, I grant you we have Kelvin Langmead in the team, but this won't go wrong. Hmmm, some grim defending lets in David Ball, a player who would prove very useful later in the season, to score. Two minutes later and Grant McCann has his once a game dawdle on the edge of the area only to be robbed of the ball and suddenly it's 3-2.

Right with 15 minutes to go to half-time any other manager in the world would have attempted to shut up shop, keep it tight and get to the break. As we would continue to find out until January, Gary Johnson was not like any other manager in the world and we continued to pile men forward in search of a goal. On the stroke of half time, Tommy Rowe made a terrible error to allow Ball in again to make it 3-3. I didn't know whether to laugh or cry, cheer or boo at this point. Thankfully the paint stripper cider offered in the Glebe bar dulled the pain for 15 minutes.

After an hour Posh score again through the genius that is George Boyd and again, stupidly, I think, right we will shut up shop now. Then Charlie waves his hand at the ball in his own penalty area and it's a penalty that Austin rattles home to make it four each. FFS, I am now fuming. This is a shambles. Deep,

deep into injury time the debacle is complete by a Swindon own goal to make it 5-4.

The ex-Cambridge munchkin then comes on the radio after the game to say: "well, we sent all the Posh fans home happy in the end". I used the next days SOTG podcast to say "Er, no Gary you f****** didn't, and proceeded to rant about the game and his management. When the podcast got released that week, Chris and I got an utter slating from the internet message boards and via e-mail, many of the messages were along the lines of: "We win and you still bloody moan" (and worse) and "How can you be miserable after a 5-4 win?" Easy mate, I am a Peterborian, born and bred.

Jamie Jones

* * * * *

23/10/10

Brentford 2 - 1 Peterborough United

Woodman '39 McCann (pen) '19
Alexander '58

Brentford: *Hamer, O'Connor, Woodman, Bean, Macdonald (sub Grabban 61min), Spillane, Weston, Wood, Osborne, Alexander, Legge. Unused subs: McCracken, Forster, Hunt, Diagouraga, Simpson, Lee.*
Posh: *Lewis, Little, Rowe (sub Nana 72min), Langmead, Zakuani, Boyd, Frecklington (sub Wesolowski 64min), McCann, Davies (sub Mendez-Laing 56min), Mackail-Smith, Mclean. Unused subs: Collis, Lee, Hibbert, Bennett.*
Attendance: *6,543 (1,149 Posh fans)*

I was a little disappointed as I had to get home at a reasonable hour from this one so I booked my train tickets in advance to get them cheaper, 'which train will the PISA lot be getting' I thought to myself, and it appeared glaringly obvious when looking at the timetable that they would be on the 08.09 out of Peterborough arriving at Kings Cross at 08.57 and thus getting to the famous New Inn in time for the 10am opening, perfect, so I booked it.

The night before Brentford away I had the usual London away day excitement building up inside. I had by now found out that the PISA lot were on a later train – for the first time ever – that would arrive over an hour after mine. I downloaded some Only Fools and Horses to my phone knowing this would keep me entertained for the journey now that I had no friends to talk to. I thought I would just check the bus timetable from Wittering to Peterborough to see what bus I would need to get. To my horror there was not one that would get me there in time so a new plan was needed.

I decided the cheapest and best solution would be to pump up my tyres and bike to Stamford to catch the 7.07 and be in Peterborough in time for my train. I could easily jump that train as there won't be a ticket inspector at that time on a Saturday. Up at 5am and I'd been warned not to wake up the kids so I tip toe around like a right prat. After successfully getting through phase 1 I look out the window - it is not cycling weather, far from it, it's absolutely pissing it down. Now it's only 5.45am and I have plenty of time to bike there but I'd be soaked so getting there on the cheap was now out of the question.

Right taxi it is, but do I get it to Peterborough for £15 or Stamford for £10? F**k it I'll go to Stamford to save a few quid as I won't get stopped on the train 'cos there won't be a ticket inspector on there at that time on a Saturday. On the train I plug in the ear phones for Del Boy episode one. Barely at the end of the theme tune and I see a shadow: "tickets please". I handed over my Mastercard to be done for nine bloody quid. The day has started terribly, it can only get better from here, can't it?

Arrive in Peterborough. Train arrives on time and it's off to London. Naturally as I actually had a ticket for this train I wasn't asked for it. On to the underground and I need my trusty phone and it's apps to tell me what line to use so that I was comfortably on time for 10am opening at The New Inn.

Arrive in Brentford and it doesn't really look that familiar. I've been loads of times but can't really remember any of them. So checked my phone again for directions and I was off. Now Mowlsey had advised me of the long walk to the New Inn but I was there in 15 minutes it must have been my longer legs and superior fitness that made the difference.

I arrive at the New Inn open the door, no one is there but the cleaners: "we don't open till twelve" they said 'TWELVE' I responded and an emergency call to the PISA Chairman revealed he was as shocked as me but said he would be there by 11 to try and resolve it.

After walking around for a mile or so I finally found a pub that was open. A couple of pints in Mr Mowles calls me: "right," he says "the New Inn is open. Mark Sheppard is in there and has been for half an hour."

"Cheeky bastards," I respond and down my pint and get down there. I walk in an order a pint, I look around but I can't see anyone so I ring the Chairman again: "Mowlsey, there is no one here mate,"

"We will be there in a minute" he responds.

Supping my beer and the phone goes again, it's Mowlsey again: "Bucks what New Inn are you in?"

"The New Inn, Brentford, obviously."

"Yeah but the cabby says there are two. Can you see the ground?"

And I have to admit I found it strange earlier that I hadn't seen the ground as I remember it being there on previous visits. I asked the barman to order me a taxi:

"Where are you going mate?"

"The other New Inn" I embarrassingly replied.

Arrived at the proper New Inn and I have to admit it looked more familiar but like I say I have only been there a dozen or so times. Anyway, it doesn't matter because I'm here now to enjoy a drink with my friends.

'Wanker, wanker, wanker' was the chant that greeted me, making me think I should've stayed at the other New Inn. Anyway, after realising I had currently spent more on unplanned travel than booze I decided it was time to hit the Jager Bombs and a few hours drinking and socialising followed.

Didn't really make too much of the first half as I was too pissed but the second half was bloody awful. This was the game when I started to doubt Johnson - later than many others - as we had no answer to a very average Brentford side.

The score and 100 odd minutes without booze was very sobering so back to the New Inn for more Jager, a moan and even more Jager. By the time we had drunk the pub dry of Jager Mowlsey had called every Posh player in his phone and sung to them. Boozy and I decided it was time to go and judging by the later footage seen of the Chairman pole-dancing on the tube we made the right call.

When you go through all the above and still enjoy your day you know you've been to Brentford away!

Craig Buckley

* * * * *

30/10/10

Peterboro' Utd 0 - 3 Brighton & Hove Albion

Barnes '16, '62
Calderón '33

Posh: *Lewis, Little, Langmead, Lee, Wesolowski (sub Nana 66min), Mclean (sub Frecklington 30min (sub Whelpdale 51min)), Boyd, McCann, Mackil-Smith, Bennett, Mendez-Laing. Unused subs: Collis, Hibbert, Piergianni, Davies.*
Brighton: *Ankergren, Greer, El-Abd, Bennett, Barnes, Calderon, Murray (sub Baz 71min), Dicker, Painter, Kishishev (sub Battipiedi 78min), Bridcutt. Subs: Brezovan, Elphick, Lua-Lua, Hart, Smith.*
Attendance: *10,116 (2,519 Brighton fans)*

October 2010

My day started strangely, and it only got stranger as the day wore on.... Firstly being kicked and harried out of the house by my wife-to-be up in Mansfield to go to watch Posh is an unusual occurrence, normally I am left with the minimum time possible to travel the 75 miles to London Road... today was going to be different though. As I took the regular drive down the A1 I received a call from my best mate and upcoming best man Jonny Head to ask if I was on time to make the 10.30am Delaine bus into Peterborough, (the plan for today was an all dayer hence the diversion to Bourne to dispose of my car). The phone call was not unusual as it is quite normal for me to be late for everything, this did not concern me. Upon arriving at my parents house I was greeted by my Dad on the doorstep asking, as I look back now some very strange questions regarding the day and Jonny hurrying me along so we would not miss the bus.

As we travelled through my lovely home town of Bourne we picked up Baldy Craig who had a rather large bag with him which I chose to ignore, Jonny was rather quiet and had his nose buried in his Iphone all the way there. As usual the first stop was the Drapers, but as this was full of gayers from Brighton we chose to divert to the Brewery Tap. At this point Jonny became quite weird and hung back from us and was on his phone a lot. Got to the Brewery Tap at 11.50am and it was shut... until 12 noon, again Jonny was being weird walking off ringing people. We were eventually let in and I was first to the bar to order a nice pint of JHB, ordered food and then.... 12.30 on the dot Jonny produced the match programme open on the page showing today's mascot. There I was resplendent in my mothers pink dressing gown drinking a bottle of Becks in a photo taken by my wife Vicki a couple of years back. I was today's mascot.

Me, 29 years old, 6 ft 5" tall, 17 stone and didn't even own a pair of football boots anymore. Nice quiet game as well, only about 3000 from Brighton coming up. As I stared at the programme in disbelief, my wife walked in with my four-year-old son Toby with his favourite Posh home shirt on, followed by a number of Posh fans and friends from Mansfield, I had been done, four months everyone and I mean everyone knew about this -Mowlesy even knew at Brentford away the weekend before and managed to keep quiet.

The duck wrap and Thai fries were left behind. I had butterflies as the taxi arrived and took Jonny, Craig and I up to London Road. We were met in reception by Dave Robertson who looks after the mascots on the day and puts them through hell on the pitch for 45 mins before kick off.

Up into the David Seaman suite for a couple of bottles of Bud for my pre-match warm up, I was then greeted by the other two mascots, from memory they were seven and eight years old, how their parents laughed when they saw me. Next was a tour around the beautiful ground that is London Road. Jonny had invited Craig and his large bag for a reason. Craig is a great photographer and he took some great pictures which Jonny put into a great album for me. The highlight of the tour was meeting the players in the changing room, Aaron Mclean was late, resulting in a £50 fine. As he walked in I asked if he fancied a photo with the mascot, he asked where he was so I said it was me to big laugh from Aaron.

Then to get changed and to get onto the pitch for the warm up and the bastards got me a kit one size too small. I then proceeded to run around for 45 mins blowing out of my arse to the amusement to my mates and my wife in the Main Stand, chants of 'you fat bastard' and 'who ate all the pies' were ringing out, I now know how Simon Rea felt for all those seasons. As 3pm approached we all went back into the tunnel where I was sweating buckets. I am sure Miss Posh was dead impressed with the fine specimen of a man I clearly am.

We had earlier been asked whom I wanted to walk out with hand in hand, I said Boydy but one of the bloody kids had got him first so I ended up with the skipper Grant McCann leading the side out. For some strange reason the home team now walk along the away team in a row shaking hands, Grant told me to lead the way… as I approached their skipper Gordon Greer I though 'christ he is a big bastard', I put my hand out to shake his and he said to me' good luck today skipper', thanks mate, he only thought I was the captain of the Posh!

Before kick off all the lads ran around high fiving, big tenning, the lot, I loved all of that, geeing them up wishing them luck…a lot of good that did. As I ran off the pitch to take my seat in the Main Stand I ran to Gary Johnson and shook his hand and wished him luck, he did a double take.

Right onto the game then… it was shit. Lost 3-0, George Boyd sent off after about 10 mins, Calderon their left back was a prick. Reluctantly I then got changed and it was off to The Beehive for some real ale and some posh crisps to drown our sorrows. A truly great day, which I will never forget.

Who would of thought promotion would have followed after that performance, shame Dmac talked Johnson out of walking out after the game… but hey we might not have had that wonderful day out at Old Trafford if he hadn't.

Pete Gout, Mansfield

* * * * *

November 2010

2/11/10

Walsall 1 - 3 Peterborough United

Gray '53 — Bennett '15, Davies '17, Langmead '55

Walsall: *Walker, Westlake, McDonald, Smith, Richards, Macken (sub Reid 71min), Taundry, Gray, McGivern, Devaney (sub Jones 77min), Dickinson. unused subs: Lescott, Lancashire, Nicholls, Marshall, Brain.*
Posh: *Lewis, Little, Nana, Langmead, Bennett, Nyatanga, Davies, Wesolowski, Tomlin, Mackail-Smith, Mclean (sub Whelpdale 85min). Unused subs: Collis, Lee, Piergianni, Hibbert, Davies, Mendez-Laing.*
Attendance: *3,294 (447 Posh fans)*

It was a bit of a shame that this season two of the best supported away days, Notts County and Walsall, were both midweek matches, but I was still expecting to see a decent turnout of Poshies in the Black Country. Sure enough, when I got to the Banks's Stadium, there was a good splash of blue wandering across the car park, and a fair few heading as usual to the Saddlers Club.

On my way to join them I was stopped by a guy with a video camera, who wanted my thoughts on the game, my score prediction, and the Posh player to look out for. I went for 2-2 I think, on the basis that Walsall were in atrocious form at the time, but on the other hand we were pretty much incapable of defending. I told him that Grant McCann was Posh's main man, despite the fact he wasn't playing, and despite a sizeable chunk of Posh fans having decided he was useless. (They may have a different opinion now, of course......)

The Saddlers Club is excellent, and the natives are among the friendliest around, but in common with most football supporters clubs, they have crap beer. As it happened, the cider

I had wasn't too clever either, but never mind. The usual suspects from Peterborough, were in residence, and after I sat down, I decided to follow their lead and get something to eat. As it was Walsall, Balti Pie and Chips was the obvious choice, so I joined the queue. It turned out that there was only a queue in the first place because of some old boy who decided to have some fun by deliberately messing about with his order, asking why they didn't have different pie fillings, moaning about the price, and generally being a right pain. Apparently he was a 'character' who did this at every game. Oh how we laughed.

I finally got my food, and went back to eat it. Once I cut into the pie, I found that I'd annoyed Adi Mowles (or is it Moys – who knows), because I had a classic balti pie, featuring generous filling and plenty of sauce. Adi, on the other hand had a pie composed pretty much of air in pastry, with just a few lumps of dry meat stuck to the bottom. Still, it'd help him get a superb physique like mine.

About that time, the coach from Bristol must have pulled in to Walsall, as Nick (Bristleposh) made his entrance. Always a style guru, he'd gone for the Argentina top, shorts and sandals. What better choice could there be for a night game in November. I got him a pint, as he'd brilliantly turned up with nothing in his wallet apart from the usual unused condom from 1971, relying instead on meeting someone who owed him money. Or me.

One more drink later, we headed into the ground. Nick looked cold; possibly the shorts were ill advised. We were on the side of the ground, with the away end left empty. Not the best arrangement for getting any sort of an atmosphere from the away fans (which is probably why Walsall went for it). Nick still looked cold.

The game itself was woeful. We won 3 – 1, with goals from the rather unlikely trio of Bennett, Davies and Langmead, because no matter how badly we played, even with Nana in the side we couldn't come close to Walsall's ineptitude. Nick looked a bit cold to me, and may by then have been regretting the sandals. At the end, the players came over to the fans to give us a clap. We clapped back, Nick relishing the chance to get some blood flowing. He looked cold, I thought. The old clichés about the sign of a good side being the ability to pick up wins when playing badly were being given an airing. Gary Johnson came over and gave us the slightly apologetic fist pumping salute we had come to expect after a win. He looked a hell of a sight warmer than Nick, though.

My journey back home to Halesowen didn't take long, so I decided to pop into the Waggon and Horses to wind down with a nice relaxing pint. Oakham seemed appropriate. As I enjoyed an Inferno, I wondered if Adi had got anything worth eating yet, considered whether Nick was still cold, and thought that there's nothing like those rare games where the Posh travel so I don't have to!

Gary Chilvers

* * * * *

06/11/10 : FA Cup

Stockport County 1 - 1 Peterborough United

Griffin '20 Mclean '28

Stockport: *Glennon, Lynch, Williams, Turnbull, Assoumani, Donnelly, Pulis, Griffin, Poole (sub Darkwah 63min), Rose, Fletcher (sub Conlon 88min). Unused subs: Vincent, Tansey, Halls, Salem, Alssop.*
Posh: *Lewis, Little, Langmead, Wesolowski, Mclean (sub Hibbert 80min), Mackail-Smith, Bennett, Davies, Nana, McCann (sub Mendez-Laing 84min) Tomlin. Unused subs: Collis, Lee, Whelpdale, Davies, Zakuani.*
Attendance: *2,001(334 away)*

This was more like it; after a season where we entered the cup with the big teams in the third round - well if you can call Spurs that – we were back on more familiar territory this year with a first round tie at Stockport.

November 2010

A crisp autumn day and after arriving at the ground far too early because I had forgotten that no one bothers with the cup now, I was approached by a man who asked me what I thought of Jim Gannon. I replied that from our experience last season I thought he was the sort of character who could start a fight in an empty room. The questioner then revealed that he was one of Stockport' directors and that Jim Gannon, was a guest at the match today. However he was being kept behind a smoked glass window for fear of the crowd reaction. I did wonder if this was because of some recently developed awful physical impairment, but it was clear that Mr Gannon was seen as brilliant football manager in these parts. I decided not to mention the CMS substitution scandal of last season, but did seek his recommendation as to the best chip shop in the area. I am pleased to say that his advice was good.

As for the match, it was rubbish. An open terrace with seats bolted on did not bode well for a cracking atmosphere amongst the 300 odd posh fans. After falling a goal behind, one Posh fan, who made Brian Blessed sound quietly spoken, bellowed out his less than positive opinion about Gary Johnson's tactical acumen. Needless to say Mr Johnson did not share this opinion. A few minutes later a number of Stockport stewards surrounded the very astute and perceptive Poshie and threw him out!

We did equalise, but the highlights of the day were certainly not the football.

Andy Smith, Chatteris

* * * * *

13/11/10

Peterborough United 1 - 5 Charlton Athletic

McCann '54	Jackson '15 (pen), '36
	Racon '25
	Martin '38, '65

Posh: *Lewis, Little, Nyatanga, Langmead, Bennett (sub Mendez-Laing 46min), Williams, Wesolowski (sub Davies 46min), McCann, Tomlin, Mclean, Mackail-Smith (sub Hibbert 46min). Unused subs: Collis, Zakuani, Piergianni, J. Davies.*
Charlton: *Elliott, Francis, Jackson, Semedo (sub Reid 87min), Wagstaff (sub McCormack 56min), Racon, Doherty, Benson, Fry, Anyinsah (sub Martin 19min), Dailly. Unused subs: Worner, Abbott, Sodje, Fortune.*
Attendance: *7,477 (1,338 Charlton fans)*

That was shyte.

Paul Donnelly

I should be writing a match report describing what happened at the game. However, going back over it in detail will only hurt too much. Today we were a disgrace. A complete and utter disgrace. I've seen some poor performances this season but none have been as bad as that was. It was a pitiful attempt from every player on the pitch. This season was supposed to be different. It was meant to be one where we won promotion back to the Championship. Again we were promised the world. The manager's appointment was supposed to have "shocked the world of football". We were meant to have a better squad than last time we were at this level. We were all set. The title was ours. And once again, just like last season, we bought into it. As a fanbase we fell for all the optimism, the promises and ultimately it looks like we are about to be let down again.

We started the campaign well. That's what worries me. When the players were trying to prove they warranted a place we looked like a fantastic, free-scoring side. Promotion looked easy. But, gradually, we have got worse. Far worse. As Johnson has influenced this team everyone has gone backwards. Today we didn't even look like we knew how to play his system. A lop-sided 3-5-2 formation, where we seemed to play without a midfield. No-one knew whether to close down or stand-off or who to mark. There was nothing. No creative spark. No defence. Just a mass of confusion.

What was Johnson's reaction? You would presume to be

shouting at his players. At least trying to get some instructions to a team who looked out of ideas from the first whistle. Instead he was a lost figure. Standing, arms behind his back, just watching. There was no reaction. He is out of ideas and doesn't know how to get this team to play.

John Verrall, www.posh.footballblog.co.uk

* * * * *

16/11/10

Peterborough United 4 - 1 Stockport County

Langmead '24	Tansey '72
Mackail-Smith '47	
Tomlin '56	
Mclean '90	

Posh: *Lewis, Little, Langmead, Zakuani. Bennett, Davies, McCann, Tomlin (sub Mendez-Laing 60min), Boyd, Mclean, Mackail-Smith (sub Hibbert 69min, sub Wesolowski 79min)). Unused subs: Collis, Piergianni, Davies, Ralph.*
Stockport: *Glennon, Lynch, Williams, Turnbull, Assoumani, Donnelly, Pulis (sub Tansey 68min), Griffin, (sub Simpson 57min) Poole, Rose, Fletcher (sub Salem 68min). Unused subs: Alssop, Vincent, Conlon, Halls.*
Attendance: *2,312 (106 Stockport fans)*

Peterborough United will travel to npower League Two side Bury in the second round of the FA Cup, sponsored by E.ON after Gary Johnson's men overcame the spirited challenge of Stockport County at London Road.

Goals from Kelvin Langmead, Craig Mackail-Smith, Lee Tomlin and Aaron Mclean earned a 4-1 victory, but it was the nasty injury to substitute striker Dave Hibbert that threatened to overshadow the Posh victory.

www.theposh.com

* * * * *

20/11/10

Southampton 4 - 1 Peterborough United

Barnard '28 — Mclean '76
Fonte '46
Chaplow '50
do Prado '80

Southampton: *Davis, Richardson, Jaidi, Fonte, Dickson, Chamberlain (sub Holmes 69min), Chaplow, Hammond, Lallana, Barnard (sub Do Prado 48min), Lambert (sub Connolly 81min). Unused subs: Bialkowski, Butterfield, Martin, Schniederlin.*
Posh: *Lewis, Little, Nyatanga, Langmead, Mclean, Boyd (sub Wesolowski 55min), McCann (sub Mendez-Laing 75min), Mackail-Smith, Davies, Tomlin (sub Clayton 55min), Williams. Unused subs: Collis, Zakuani, Bennett, Davies.*
Attendance: *22,177 (1016 Posh fans)*

Writing a derogatory match report after the club has just won promotion to the Championship feels somewhat bizarre. But the sparkling achievement at Old Trafford provides a perfect juxtaposition to the dark days of November, when defending was a stranger and CMS was still 23 goals away from hero status.

Having been thrashed 5-1 at home by Charlton the previous Saturday there was little confidence amongst Posh fans in the week before the trip to St Mary's, there was none as far as I was concerned.

The MD of the company where I work is a life-long Saints fan and we arranged to meet up before the match in a pub about 15 minutes walk from the ground. The Royal Oak, near the redundant East Docks, conjoured images of hard-drinking dockers sporting weather-beaten features and callused hands. In fact it's a 60s pub underneath a piss-stained multi-storeyed car park. Saints fans packed the premises and my glasses fogged instantly as the cold lenses met the steamy interior.

Pint in hand and vision restored I wandered around until I found my boss. Like everyone else he was wearing this season's new white shirt with its diagonal red stripe. It reminded me of the Peru shirt from Argentina '78, an absolute classic, and he appreciated my genuine appreciation for the design. We discussed the game's prospects and he was shocked to hear my pessimistic 4-1 prediction. Saints had started the season badly, winning only one game in their first seven, by contrast Posh had started well and were eight points in front at that time. Now, nine games later, they were just one point ahead.

St Mary's is an impressive stadium for League One. We sat in the away end, in the opposite corner to the thousand-strong Posh following. As the teams ran out I felt a pang of trepidation; Posh looked small and insignificant inside this bowl, whereas Southampton strode around with complete confidence.

Posh had two loanees at the back, Lewin Nyatanga and Marcus Williams, partnering Little and Langmead and another two loanees on the bench, including midfielder Adam Clayton who had just signed from Leeds. After ten minutes I was gobsmacked we were still in the game. Every time wingers Oxlade-Chamberlain and Lallana touched the ball I had to watch through my fingers as we rolled around like drunken sailors.

But we survived and settled down to play some decent football through midfield. There was even time for CMS to miss his weekly one-on-one before the wheels fell off and Lee Barnard smashed home a shot from the edge of the area. One-nil down at the break was a fantastic achievement given the tidal flow of possession in favour of the home team. We left our seats for a half time drink then trundled down to the home end to watch Act Two.

Five minutes later Posh were 3-0 down and I was cursing my apparently optimistic score prediction. The second half passed in a blur to be honest. Saints passed the ball around smoothly and threatened to score at will, fortunately Joe Lewis was having a blinder. NML had a shot from the edge of the area that went out for a throw in, it was that bad. Aaron notched with fifteen to go, but there was no hope of a comeback and five minutes later Saints delivered the fourth.

On the drive home I seriously contemplated relegation. Posh were now closer to the drop zone than promotion, but I reassured myself that the squad would get better with time. Later that night I wrote on LondonRoad.net that we needed to realign our expectations. "There is no way on God's green earth that this squad will achieve promotion." I said. It was that depressing.

Three days later an article in the Sun claimed Darragh had given Tragic Johnson five games to turn the season around. He lasted six.

Phil Keys, Animal Kingdom

* * * * *

23/11/10

Peterborough United 2 - 2 Leyton Orient

Mclean '18 (pen), '61	Revell '43
	Smith '86

Posh: *Lewis, Little, Langmead, Wesolowski, Mclean, Boyd, Bennett, Davies (sub Mendez-Laing 88min), Tomlin, Williams, Clayton. Unused subs: Collis, Nyatanga, Zakuani, Rowe, J. Davies, Ralph.*
Leyton Orient: *Brown, Omozusi, Whing (sub M'Poku 46min), Brown, Forbes, Cox, Revell (sub Walker 88min), Daniels, Spring, Tehoue (sub McGleish 72min), Smith. Unused subs: Butcher, Jarvis, Cestor, Millwood.*
Attendance: *4,423 (351 Orient fans)*

It was a quick dash from work to get to the ground to meet up with my mates on a cold Tuesday night. I always like night games as the atmosphere is different to a Saturday; more electric.

I can't say I was confident, without CMS and his energy I thought we might struggle. But with Tomlin firing wide not long onto the game I changed my mind and thought three points might be on the cards. Shortly after Boyd was fouled in the area and Aaron Mclean stepped up to score from the spot. There was the usual jumping for joy on the terraces, but also nervousness because under Gary Johnson we struggled to hold onto a lead.

Our defence looked nervous every time Orient attacked and just before half time they got their reward through Revell and it was 1-1. 15 minutes into the second-half Posh were back in the lead with Mclean scoring again. But we needed another goal to make the game safe because of our ropey defence.

But as full-time approached Orient equalised. I couldn't believe it and my heart sank. Into stoppage time and Tomlin tumbled to the ground in the area and another penalty was given. I stood waiting to jump for joy as surely Mclean was get his hat trick and give Posh three points. But it was saved. Absolutely gutted as the game ended 2-2. Walking away from the stadium I tried to keep positive as we hadn't lost, but though it was a point gained it felt like two points dropped.

Aaron Knighton

* * * * *

27/11/10

Bury 1 - 2 Peterborough United

Lowe '51 — Tomlin '13, Mackail-Smith '38

Bury: *Fon Williams, Picken (sub Worrall 79min), Skarz, Lees, Sweeney (sub John-Lewis 85min), Haworth (sub Carlton 90min), Jones, Lowe, Sodje, Ajose, Wallace. Unused subs: Worrall, Bennett, Gunning, Branagan, Harrop.*

Posh: *Lewis, Langmead, Zakuani, Wesolowski, Mclean (sub Little 83min), Boyd, McCann (sub Davies 90min), Mackail-Smith, Rowe, Bennett, Tomlin. Unused subs: Piergianni, Mendez-Laing, Collis, J. Davies.*

Attendance: *2,514 (186 Posh fans)*

By golly, by jeez, up at a good time for a F.A. Cup 2nd Round tie away at glamorous Bury of 'Division Four' at their Gigg Lane Ground. And it was cold, very cold in Peterborough and with Bury very much nearer the North Pole it is going to be even colder up there.

We all huddled together in a group on the Moy's End Car Park awaiting the Coach and the anticipated warm comfort inside. The usual crowd of diehards that never let the Club down included Nipper, Ashman, Gobber, Paul.M, Alan.B, Norman and 'ol Jack B etc to name just a few discussed the game to come, the Coach was just about full. As we set off once again for the North of Manchester and guessing the A1 ,then the M62 and across today an even bleaker than usual Saddleworth Moor. I got called a nut job on a message board for going to Bury but when has anyone on there been right except me? Bury lay third in their division, were playing well and with our inconsistency a banana skin loomed.

As we travelled North the amount of snow and ice laying around increased and some doubts crept in but Gigg Lane had assured us it was on after covering the pitch for the previous couple of days. On arrival we selected a nearby Pub, had a drink or two and met several other fans that always travel when we are in that area from and are always a pleasure to talk to for yet another view on our beloved Posh. No aggro encountered just friendly banter with the locals when we joined the crowd that in the end amounted to a massive 2,514.

Plenty of room to move about: a great choice, to stand, to sit or move away from anyone you did not want to sit near. Perfect but by golly it was cold, and getting colder. For the first time this ol' man questioned himself and his sanity: 'what the hell are you doing at 74 years old' following Posh in conditions that only Capt. Scott/Oates would've considered suitable. The cold compared with, if not beat, the Cup Replay night at Burton Albion when Carden gave me a personal V sign at the end of the game for too loudly venting my feelings on their overall pathetic performance.

It was an energetic and enjoyable first half. A great team performance in which we defended from the front right to the back. Bury were not in it and Tomlin shone like a beacon but the team as a whole all performed together. A great pass from McCann to CMS, then again onto Tomlin saw us take the lead after just 13 minutes. Another from Craig Mackail-Smith himself after 39 minutes and the cockles of our hearts were beginning to warm. We were in control and remained so until half time.

Whatever Gary Johnson said to them at half time turned them off and we were back to indifference and nail biting especially so when Bury scored after 50 minutes. We had stopped backing each other up, energy levels dropped by a unit of 10 and we gave them so much more space. Gradually and slowly though we shook ourselves out of our complacent mood and began to dig in, and by some grit and determination got ourselves playing some decent football again. The pitch by now began to freeze over and it became slippery and led to mistakes by both sides but we held on and Bury faded towards the end. The final whistle sounded and we were through. Craig had now scored 12 F.A. Cup goals beating Jim Halls's record of 11.

Lewis had a cracking game and had maybe done more than anyone to get us through. Tomlin had a great first half and George Boyd as usual worked his socks off. We still looked at times very fragile in defence and the next Round v Fulham at Craven Cottage(drawn the next day)would show up just how vulnerable. At the end though we felt it could just restart our season in the League as we were now at our lowest position all season, 12th.

Our journey home did not seem quite so long - it never does when you win - and the chatter was at a normal crescendo, totally opposite to when we lose and we hide behind our books and programmes. I had my usual half-hour nap complete with snoring on the Coach but have to say it was good to arrive home and to a warm house.

Special mention again must be made about the 186 diehard Posh fans who turned out on a day when even the cat and dog preferred a cosy chair inside, but hey! that is what it is all about, is it not?

You did us proud in the end Posh players, and fans, and now to Fulham.

Brian Seaton

* * * * *

December 2010

10/12/10

Peterborough United 2 - 1 Rochdale

Mclean '19 Akpa Akpro '70
Mackail-Smith '50

Posh: *Lewis, Little, Langmead, Zakuani, Rowe, Clayton, McCann, Boyd (sub Piergianni 90min), Tomlin (sub Mendez-Laing 90min), Mclean, Mackail-Smith. Unused subs: Collis, Wesolowski, Davies, Nana, Williams.*
Rochdale: *Daniels, Wiseman, Holness, Kennedy, Jones, Done, Grant (sub Elding 53min), O'Grady, Kennedy, Dawson, Adams (sub Akpro 53min). Unused subs: Widdowson, Barry-Murphy, Thompson, Gray.*
Attendance: *4,233 (134 Rochdale fans)*

Football on a Friday is not my cup of tea - a march through Peterborough the next day having caused the switch – as the result can make or break your weekend before it has even started.

A work day along with rubbish traffic on a Friday afternoon all add to the stress of whether I can get there on time. Especially as I have to travel to the game from Coventry via Huntingdon to pick up my partner in crime Pete - aka the prowler. On time of course means 6pm – well, its tradition.

Having sworn at plenty of motorists on the journey slowing me down we arrive safely in Charters for 5.55pm. A couple of Oakham ales followed by a truly awesome chilli kebab from Curryland and I'm ready for action.

As I reach step out onto the upper tier of the South Stand I am taken aback by the massed ranks of the 134 Rochdale fans. Let's be fair, these are true football fans and are the lifeblood of our game. Mind you the South stand did not seem to have too many more in either - it transpired that this was the lowest league crowd of the season – that's Friday football for you !

Remember this game was before Fergie came back so what do we do? 2-0 up - obligatory MacAttack goal each - and we should be cruising only to allow them back into the match by defending like schoolkids, conceding a goal and getting battered for the last ten minutes as we just hold on. The three points taking us up to eighth in the table

What of course we did not know at the time was that this was the last time we'd see Mclean in a Posh shirt. I remember Aaron's debut in October 2006 against Swansea in the JPT and will never forget the amazing impact he had. Never stopped smiling and never stopped running. His tally of 29 League goals in 45 games in 2007/8 season will live long in the memory .He was the first of the Darragh revolution signings and to me, is a true Posh legend.

Anyway - the weekend was already a memorable one and it was only 9.40pm Friday.

David Gibbons

* * * * *

28/12/10

Swindon Town 1 - 1 Peterborough United

Austin '72 (pen) Tomlin '19

Swindon: *Smith, Cuthbert, Frampton, Caddis, McGovern, Ferry, Pericard (sub Dossevi 62min), Prutton, Sheehan, Ritchie (sub O'Brien 86min), Austin. Unused subs: Scott, Rose, Timlin, Morrison, Ball.*
Posh: *Lewis, Little, Langmead, Zakuani, Boyd, McCann (sub Wesolowski 77min), Mackail-Smith, Rowe, Whelpdale (sub Lee 68min), Tomlin (sub Mendez-Laing 67min), Clayton. Unused subs: Collis, Bennett, Davies, Nana.*
Attendance: *8,519 (440 Posh fans)*

There aren't many things that would make me leave temperatures of 30 degrees plus to experience the freezing temperatures that our fine country enjoys in December. However, it's what my good friend Dan, who spent a few months of the 2008-2009 season living in Sugar Way before returning to Western Australia, decided to do as he was desperate to come over and watch the Posh again.

He travelled from Perth via New York in time for the Swindon game at the County Ground. He had his flights booked, transport arranged to get him from Gatwick to Swindon and his Posh shirt packed. All was looking OK until vast amounts of snow decided to fall on the Eastern Coast of the US shutting all of New York's airports just as he was about to depart. To say he was disappointed was an understatement. Well there's always next year.

The weather in the UK during December hadn't been much better than New York with leading to a number of Posh's games being postponed and 18 days had passed since Posh last played - Rochdale at home. On londonroad.net even some of the Posh elders had declared that they weren't going to buy a Swindon ticket due to the stack of tickets they had at home from the postponed games. Swindon even cast doubt on the game going ahead by putting a message on their website asking for volunteers to help clear the snow on the morning of the 27th. It promised to be a low turnout.

Even though the weather was poor and the game far from certain to go ahead we set off for Swindon. My ever-cautious dad, concerned about the prospect of snow and the potential of slow progress, decided we should leave excessively early. Having a spare ticket we set about convincing someone to brave the Arctic conditions and join us for the game. Having spent my early years growing up in Wiltshire at least meant that it wasn't going to be hard to encourage a friend to come along and watch a free game of football. I was proven right and a small detour via Lechlade meant that our spare ticket was now allocated.

Even with the detour we still arrived in Swindon at about 11am. Hungry but way too early to approach the ground we decided to seek out some food and with the local knowledge of our passenger we decided on a pleasant £4.99 all you can eat Chinese buffet. We spent the next couple of hours consuming enough Pork Balls, Chow Mein and Crispy Shredded Beef to feed a small army. Uncomfortably full we set off in the direction of the County Ground. Our local expert directed us to a Lidl with no parking restrictions and a quick exit after the game. The only downside, which he had failed to mention, was that it was about two miles to the County Ground. Oh well, at least we got a chance to burn off some of that MSG.

Walking past the main stand at the County Ground Messrs Fry and MacAnthony were seen deep in discussion outside the executive lounge, possibly about how to spend the funds they were about to receive from Mclean's transfer to Hull.

We made our way into the ground and were informed that the Posh coach had been held up due to the weather and kick off had been delayed by 15 mins....if only they had listened to my dad.

The players were out warming up, Mclean-less, just in front of us. Tomlin didn't look a well man and was coughing like he smoked 50 a day (we later heard that he had a severe chest infection). CMS was the model professional and after warming up posed for photos with fans and signed autographs. An older gent wandered down to the front and got a hug from CMS leading to my dad instantly declaring it must have been his granddad (a rumour that continues to be completely unsubstantiated)

The game finally kicked off at 15:20 with Whelpdale restored to the starting line up after returning from a loan spell at Gillingham. Posh started confidently, playing some good football and moving the ball around well. Whelpdale, CMS and Langmead all went close whilst at the other end Lewis saved comfortably from Charlie Austin. After 17 minutes Boyd turned well and played in Tomlin who used his strength to drill the ball into the bottom corner of the goal. Posh continued to have the better of the first half but possibly affected by the 18 days without a competitive game couldn't get that elusive second.

Half time arrived with temperatures rapidly approaching zero. This would normally be a perfect time to get a warm drink but the effects of the Chinese buffet were still apparent and we felt unable to move.

The second-half kicked off, with Swindon having much the better of it. Lewis was tested by Pericard and Sheehan, the latter effort really getting the Town fans behind their team. Tomlin and Whelpdale went off to be replaced by NML and Lee. Then the breakthrough for Swindon, Little's challenge on Ritchie was judged to be unfair and a penalty awarded. Prolific marksmen Charlie Austin stepped up and converted. The impetus was very much with Swindon and Austin looked to have won the game for Swindon in stoppage time when he put the ball in the net, but fortunately he handled in the build up - a big let off.

The game had failed to live up to the excitement of the 5-4 game at London Road earlier in the season and finished at 1-1. The effect on the team of the extreme wintry conditions and 18 day gap since the last game was apparent to the 440 Posh fans that had braved the conditions.

The journey home is why, rather perversely, I like going to football in the winter. That feeling of thawing out whilst listening to Sports Report and 606 on the journey home can't be beaten, even though we continued to feel uncomfortably full and the bad weather made a two hour journey take at least twice that long.

Stuart Gilham, St.Ives

* * * * *

January 2011

03/01/11

Peterborough United 4 - 1 Walsall

Mackail-Smith '36, '71 Nicholls '10
Mendez-Laing '81
Bennett '90

Posh: *Lewis, Little, Langmead, Zakuani, McCann, Mackail-Smith, Rowe, Whelpdale (sub Mendez-Laing 71min), Davies (sub Wesolowski 79min), Tomlin (sub Bennett 84min), Clayton. Unused subs: Collis, J. Davies, Mills.*
Walsall: *Brain, Westlake, Lescott, Lancashire, Jones (sub Paterson 84min), Richards, Nicholls, Gray, Reid (sub Macken 76min), Butler. Unused subs: Bevan, McDonald, Smith, Grigg, McIvern.*
Attendance: *5,517 (142 Walsall fans)*

This was my first game of the season. The wounds of the Fergie, Cooper, Gannon debacle of the previous season still ached when it rained and I was a little less in love with Posh than I'd been before.

I was joined at the game by my brother-in-law Justin and my nephews Dominic and Jeremy who were over from South Africa for Christmas. Their flights in had coincided with all that wrong type of snow falling on Heathrow, they'd been delayed in Munich for 48 hours and Lufthansa had lost all their luggage and so I thought I'd complete their misery by forcing them to come to London Road with me.

The last, and only, games of football they had previously been to were Brazil v Portugal and Germany v Australia in the 2010 World Cup. So no pressure on Posh to entertain then. London Road was reassuringly ramshackle, the tea was awful and it was 'kin freezing. Classic Posh.

It was an odd game. The least convincing 4-1 victory I think I've ever seen. I don't think our midfield won a tackle all game and fan favourite Langmead seemed loathe to move any further forward than the edge of our 18 yard box – and the Walsall strikers were still getting in behind him.. It was all very flat, very unconvincing.

Walsall's goal was the result of a free header and they looked capable of scoring each time they attacked. Unfortunately for them they were absolutely atrocious at the back and CMS, despite spurning a couple of chances, always looked likely to score.

Posh equalised and then in the second-half kept plugging to away before scoring three more scoreline-flattering goals late on. Teflon Joe pulled off a couple of good saves – in particular one from Macken late on – and was handed the man-of-the-match award

My nephews, well brought-up polite boys that they are, said they enjoyed it. Their highlight – the crowd singing cheerio to the Walsall assistant-manager after he was sent to the stands. Thanks to the vuvuzela it was the first time they had heard a crowd sing at a football match.

Paul Mitchell

* * * * *

08/01/11 : FA Cup 3rd Round

Fulham FC 6 - 2 Peterborough United

Kamara '32, '59, '76	Tomlin '71
Ethuhu '45	McCann '86
Gera '66	
Greening '89	

Fulham: *Stockdale, Pantsil, Hangeland (sub Halliche 77min), Baird, Murphy, Kamara, Duff, Hughes, Etuhu, Dempsey (sub Greening 62min), Davies (sub Gera 46min). Unused subs: Etheridge, Salcido, Riise, Johnson.*

Posh: *Lewis, Little, Langmead, Zakuani, Rowe, Whelpdae (sub Mendez-Laing 46min), Davies (sub Obika 57min), Clayton (sub Agard 69min), McCann, Tomlin, Mackail-Smith. Unused subs: Collis, Bennett, Nana, Wesolowski.*
Attendance: *15,936 (4,609 Posh fans)*

At last something to take our minds off the rigours of a league campaign where the pressure on the team and manager was beginning to build as the Posh fans became increasingly concerned at our leaky defence and inability to consolidate an automatic promotion place. Whilst the FA Cup may have lost some of its magic an away day at a premiership club is always something to look forward to. Being an ex soldier, advance military planning was required to ensure that the weekend was enjoyed to the full and with this in mind we locked ourselves away for the evening to ensure nothing was left to chance.

First action was transportation – a train up to the smoke after work on the Friday evening was booked, with the arrival due at 9pm and a return home the Saturday evening after the game.

Secondly; a place to lay our heads that evening and the new Travelodge at Waterloo fitted the bill....no trek across London and close to pubs and eateries. Now the only problem left was tickets. Always a challenge; but fortunately plenty were made available at a knock down price so no need to call in any favours from locally based Poshies.

Friday arrived and off we set, with a 3 hour journey ahead we passed the time working our way through a case of lager and some nibbles before arriving in London in good time. A stroll to the Travelodge to drop off the back packs and then an even swifter stroll back up to the pub to sink a couple more lemonades before calling into the nearest Indian for the obligatory curry before bed.

The following day dawned and the weather was decidedly fresh – we decided that a stroll all along the Thames was in order to blow away the cobwebs of the night before. All along the embankment, past Chelsea and on towards Putney Bridge and Fulham...it was a bloody long way. At last we reached Putney Bridge tube and found a great cafe for a late breakfast....the pub next door was resounding to chants of Boro....Boro but we resisted – we had somewhere else in mind. Over Putney Bridge and onto the Bricklayers Arms – what a find. With a huge number of real ales on show, warm fires and packed with fans of both clubs we started to sample what was on offer. Two hours later and suitably refreshed it was time again to stroll in the crisp winter sunshine to The Cottage.

Craven Cottage...a bit shabby round the edges but a nice old ground in a London Road type of way. Sadly it was bereft of Fulham fans who preferred the warmth of their centrally heated homes to the excitement of the cup. Posh, however, were there in great numbers and soon the away end began to fill up. Teams were announced and it was great to hear that Fulham would field a strong side which included former Posh favourite Simon Davies. As kick off approached the Posh faithful began to find their voice. Could we pull of a shock result and really set our season alight?

With Boyd and Lee unavailable due to injury would we really have the skill and passion needed to turn these premiership boys over? Loan signings Agard and Obika ,both young premiership hopefuls, were on the bench so maybe they would be the one's to write a bit of history. Out came the teams to a great roar of appreciation from the 4,000 in the away end. For once Posh started very brightly, determined to get stuck in and push for the early goal. For the first 10 minutes it was all Posh as we dictated the game and forced a good number of corners with a couple of early chances falling to CMS and Davies. The early excitement faded as Fulham began to play a bit and Simon Davies went close as we began to struggle with their wide players.

On the half-hour a cross from the right to the back post saw Kamara power in with a fine header to put Fulham ahead. 1–0

Fulham. The signs were not good as Fulham now began to push hard and the quality began to show and just on half time Duff pulled the ball back for Etuhu to bury it in the back of the net. 2–0 Fulham.

The first half over and to be fair to Posh we had shown glimpses of quality in attack but defensively it was obvious that we were struggling badly to contain the crisp passing and movement of a good Fulham side. Our full backs were exposed and were being beaten far too often...the signs were not good. Still it was the cup and who knows what could happen.

Again Posh came out of the blocks sharper as the second period commenced and Mendez–Laing began to find space and CMS put a header wide following a McCann corner. But the flicker of hope faded as Duff hit the post and then minutes later Kamara raced clear to slot home there third and kill the tie. 3 – 0 Fulham. No point in hanging back now and as Posh pushed forward gaps as wide as the Grand Canyon appeared in our defence every time Fulham counter attacked. We all knew more goals were coming. Another deep cross and header saw Fulham's fourth goal nestle in the back of the net. 4–0 Fulham.

This was now beginning to hurt a bit and Posh needed to respond quickly if this was not to get worse. Step up Lee Tomlin who raced forward beating his man and easing the ball into the net. At last something to cheer. Despite the score Posh fans were in fine voice encouraging the team to press forward and do what we do best – attack. Posh were working very hard trying to match the passing and movement of the premiership side and at times we did reach their level. However, inevitably the pace of the Fulham forwards caught Posh out and they carved us open again and with Lewis exposed they put away number five. 5–1 Fulham. Gary Johnson's last throw of the dice was to bring on Obika and almost immediately he had his chance but failed to make it count. It was up to that man CMS to cause havoc and panic in the Fulham defence resulting in a penalty which captain McCann coolly put away.

Resigned to defeat the travelling Poshies were determined to enjoy the day and PUFC resounded around the ground, followed by we will win 6 -5 J. Credit to Posh we never gave up and should have pulled another back with a Langmead header but it was not to be. The *coup de gras* happened moments later as Little was easily beaten by Greening and goal number six was put away. 6–2 Fulham. The referee bought the game to a close and despite being dumped out of the cup we did give it a go and the team got a good send off as they left the pitch.

Time now to make our way back to Waterloo station for the journey home – yes we had played well for brief parts of the game but defensively we were miles away, a problem to which Gary Johnson seemingly had no solution. Based on this performance there was little chance of Posh returning to the Championship anytime soon.

John Middleton

* * * * *

11/01/11

Gary Johnson dramatically walked out on Posh last night after just nine months in charge at London Road. The manager left after failing to agree on future club policy matters with chairman Darragh MacAnthony. MacAnthony will today start a search for his fifth Posh manager in the last 15 months.

Johnson took training as normal yesterday and picked his team to face Brentford before speaking to the press about the match. He conducted a phone interview with The Evening Telegraph at 4pm and gave no indication that his future at Posh was in doubt.

The brief club statement will invite speculation as to the particular policy details which prompted such a dramatic course of action.MacAnthony has already angrily denied accusations aired on national radio last night that he had been heard delivering dressing downs to players after poor performances. But it's known that manager and chairman have had disagreements on transfer policy in the past. MacAnthony was scathing in his criticism of defenders Lewin Nyatanga and Marcus Williams after they were brought in on loan earlier this season.

Johnson also admitted that he had quit at half-time of the home defeat by Brighton in October, although that was more to do with doubts about his own ability to motivate the current squad. Nontheless he had to be persuaded to stay on by Posh director of football Barry Fry and chief executive Bob Symns after that match.

Alan Swann, The Evening Telegraph

* * * * *

11/01/11

Peterborough United 2 - 1 Brentford

McCann (pen) '5 Laird '74
Obika '90

Posh: *Lewis, Little, Zakuani (sub Langmead 16min), Boyd, McCann, Mackail-Smith, Rowe, Bennett, Whelpdale (sub Mendez-Laing 79min), Tomlin (sub Obika 52min), Clayton. Unused subs: Collis, Wesolowski, Agard, Nana.*
Brentford: *Lee, O'Connor, Woodman, Bean, Balkenstein, MacDonald, Weston, Spillane, Osborne, Laird, Alexander (sub Forster 79min). Unused subs: Royce, McCracken, Diagouraga, Simpson, Wright, Bush.*
Attendance: *4,667 (186 Brentford fans)*

David Oldfield. His record as Posh Manager: Played one, won one. Win ratio: 100 per cent. In a day that will go down in Posh folklore as dominated by the tale of two managers, the man who managed us to victory that day wasn't one of them.

A crazy 48 hours in Posh's history started for me when I logged on to Londonroad.net at midnight the day before the game. Anticipating sifting through the usual thread of score and team predictions to whet my appetite for the match, as I signed in the first thread to pop up was titled 'Odds on next manager'. Very bizarre I thought. The only explanation I could think of was maybe there were rumours about Gary Johnson quitting again? He couldn't have been sacked. He just couldn't have.

The reason why I refused to believe Johnson had left was quite simply everything that had been said by everyone at the club since last season. In the Championship Darragh had been panicked by the lack of success and started sacking managers left, right and centre. We were assured this would never happen again. Darragh promised no matter how troubled the waters, he and the manager would stay the course. The buzzword of the season was stability.

I clicked on the thread. It was true. The impossible had happened, Gary Johnson had left the club by mutual consent.

I was stunned, and angry. I hadn't been the biggest fan of Johnson's management, but had believed Darragh when he told us the club needed stability. For him to be sacked mid-season with us sitting just outside of the play-offs was, I believed, frankly ludicrous. Everyone knew we had big ambitions for the season, and maybe the team weren't living up to potential, but how many teams sack a manager half way in to the season and get promoted? More importantly who the hell were we going to find that's better?

It had been two hours since the news had broken and the internet forums had gone mental. Shock, anger and bewilderment were the main emotions people were feeling. The whole season had been plunged in to chaos with one announcement. However, it didn't take long for attention to turn to who was coming to rescue it.

Some realistic names were mentioned, some unrealistic. Then one clever sod put two and two together. "Darren Ferguson left Preston only a few weeks ago." Suddenly every other post was Fergie, Fergie, Fergie. No, Yes, No, Yes, No. Surely it couldn't happen. At 4am, I finally dragged myself away from the screen and put my weary head down for the night.

I awoke the next day to find Ferguson as odds on favourite to be the next Posh manager, and still no explanation from the club as to why Gary Johnson had left. Added to this drama was the fact there was a match tonight, which if we won would put us in the play-off places, and which we would have to play manager-less. It was going to be a crazy day.

The Ferguson rumours continued throughout the day until, in the early afternoon, bookmakers stopped taking bets on it. It was obviously a done deal, but I still couldn't believe it.

At 5pm, I left for the match with my ears pressed firmly to Radio Cambs. Gary Johnson was on. Maybe we'd get some answers. He said it was a failure to get on with the owner and they had agreed it would be better to part ways. So essentially a sacking, albeit a nice one. Hearing him talk I felt sorry for him, and whilst maintaining he could have done a better job, I thought he was very unlucky to get the boot. Then the big news was announced: Darren Ferguson was going to be at London Road tonight.

Eating a pre-match curry in the pub my dad and I chewed over the fat of Fergie's return. It seemed such a crazy turn of events. After that wet night in November 2009 when, under accusations of bust-ups and tapping-up, Fergie had driven out of London Road for good, there had been a stream of vitriol aimed at him from some fans and club figures. His commitment and, since his move to Preston, his ability as a manger had been questioned by many fans. After hearing the club's version of events I too was hostile towards him, which is some feat considering he was a double promotion winning manager. But, it seemed, he was back. I wasn't happy but I wasn't angry. Ambivalence all round then.

Fully fed we wandered down to the ground. There seemed an air of tension around London Road that night, which made me all the more anxious for the match ahead. David Oldfield was to be the manager and he named a similar team to the one that started the last league match. Steady as she goes.

After five minutes the Posh were 1-0 up. George Boyd was brought down in the area and McCann chipped home the resultant penalty. An early goal was no surprise, but now Johnson had left could we start to hold on to a lead? The only other notable thing about the first half was some of my fellow London Road Enders singing "Fergie give us a wave". I didn't join in, I wasn't sure how I felt about his return, but I wasn't overjoyed. He gave them a wave.

In the second half we came under increasingly heavy pressure, with Lewis making a few excellent saves, before at last we buckled. A curling shot was tipped on to the post before a Brentford player poked home the rebound with his knee. The manager may be different, but everything else is the same, I thought to myself.

In the final ten minutes we threw everything at the Brentford goal and nothing stuck. Until finally in the 94th minute up stepped Jonathan Obika, in his second, and last, Posh appearance to deflect a Mackail-Smith overhead kick into the Brentford net. An improbable hero for an improbable day. Behind the goal we went mad. We'd done it again.

The final whistle went. We filed out singing and headed for home.

The future was as uncertain as ever, but we were back in the play-off places. And, perhaps, just a touch happier than 90 minutes earlier.

Chris Chapman. Soham

* * * * *

12/01/11

Darren Ferguson's sensational return to London Road will be confirmed this morning. Ferguson, who left London Road in acrimonious circumstances in November 2009, agreed a two-and-a-half year contract with chairman Darragh MacAnthony yesterday.

He will be formally unveiled as Posh boss at a London Road press conference at 10.30am today. Ferguson and MacAnthony watched last night's League One clash with Brentford together just 24 hours after Gary Johnson was relieved of his managerial duties.

Ferguson's appointment will herald a remarkable turnaround in the relationship between manager, chairman and the club's director of football Barry Fry.

Alan Swann, The Evening Telegraph

* * * * *

15/01/11

Brighton & Hove Albion 3- 1 Peterboro' United

Wood '25, '55 Tomlin '66
Bennett '27

Brighton: *Ankergren, Greer, El-Abd, Bennett, Sparrow (sub Kishishev 73min), Calderon, Murray (sub Barnes 78min), Painter, Bridcutt, Noone (sub Dicker 61min), Wood. Unused subs: Brezovan, Elphick, Holroyd, Sandaza.*
Posh: *Lewis, Langmead, Lee, Boyd, McCann, Mackail-Smith, Rowe, Bennett, Whelpdale, Tomlin, Clayton (sub Wesolowski 58min). Unused subs: Little, Agard, Mendez-Laing, Nana, Collis, Obika.*
Attendance: *7,233 (248 Posh fans)*

When 10am sets off an alarm in a student bedroom, you know something very important must be happening.

Many great dynasties have humble beginnings. Rome was founded by a couple of shepherds and an oddly maternal wolf, and Darren Ferguson's second reign as Posh boss started on the south coast in a stadium with more sides than drunken dodecahedron.

The day before the match I had listened to Darragh MacAnthony's excellent interview with the *Standing on the*

Glebe podcast. As enthusiastic as ever Darragh had convinced me that Posh were on the way up, we were going to smash Brighton 5-0 and that I could walk through walls (which I can't. I eventually gave up trying and just bought a ticket like everyone else). The man could sell an eskimo to a polar bear, which is some achievement as I always assumed polar bears had no understanding of the concept of ownership. I believed once more.

And so off we set, my father and I for the home of Gus Poyet's league leaders. The trains were only running as far as Crawley and so after a brief explanation to my nonplussed dad that this was a problem as Brighton, in fact, played in Brighton rather than Crawley, we jumped in the car and set off down the A11.

After just over two two hours of pleasantly smooth driving and a stop for a donut and some coffee we arrived on the outskirts of Brighton and saw a sign for the matchday park and ride. The service turned out just to be a very long road that was shut on matchdays on which everyone parked. None-the-less, a bus was there waiting and it was free so it seemed a tidy little operation.

After the windy and needlessly long bus ride came to an end, we were finally at the ground. Brighton was apparently one of the only grounds in the country to have a pub attached to the ground, which was exciting. Too exciting for some as the burning question didn't take long to leave my dad's lips as he accosted the bus driver: "Oi! Where's the pub?" Straight in front of us was the answer and so we headed inside. Some local beer and one nice cider for the driver (dad, not the bus driver) later, we left the warm, welcoming pub to venture to the away end of what I was later informed that due to being sited at the bottom of two big hills is one of the coldest grounds in Britain. And it was bloody cold enough that day to begin with!

Not surprisingly only 248 Poshies made the journey down. However those that did were to receive handsome reward before kick-off when that bald bloke from the Football League Show turned up. "Who's that?" I was asked, a question presumably mirrored amongst most of the travelling contingent. He asked us if we had a song or something for Fergie that they could get on tape. A few people in the middle of the stand responded with a poorly co-ordinated rendition of 'Darren Ferguson's blue and white army', the rest of us looked on with neutral expressions. I couldn't help but see this as a microcosm of the reaction to Fergie's return. Some were over the moon, some were outright hostile. However, the majority were apprehensive and basically unsure what to think. Could it be as good as the first time? Was all the animosity really water under the bridge? Was he even that good of a manager? And does Barry Fry really ask for his 10% to be paid in children's souls? Uncertainty reigned as we awaited the first sight of our prodigal son.

Fergie and the team emerged out of the tunnel to warm applause and the usual chants of 'Boro!' Any inclinings of disquiet were silenced. No matter who was in charge, who was on the pitch, or where we were playing, the most important thing was we were all there to support PUFC. It's Posh We Are after all.

The game itself wasn't bad at all. After a bright start from Posh, a mix up between Ryan Bennett and Lewis at the near post allowed Brighton to take the lead from a low cross. Shortly afterwards the hapless tackling of the Posh midfield and the inept attempt at a block by centre-half extrodinare Kelvin Langmead (our best guess was that we was trying to imitate a starfish) combined to put Brighton 2-0 up before the break.

At half-time a few people went out back for a fag and were quickly told that they were in a no smoking stadium. In spite of being a non-smoker I felt this was just like the argument over standing that had been raging between fan and steward all of the first-half. In a stand made from concrete and plastic, and more open to the elements than a naked chemist, there was no reason not to let people smoke at the back of the stand.

Likewise in a stand made for 1,000 people, but currently only housing 200 why not let people stand if they want to? After a sarcastic remark or two the steward who informed me it was a rule imposed as part of their lease of the ground. Fair enough.

Thus followed a very informative conversation with the steward where I heard the problems they had been having with homophobia (which is still worryingly commonplace in football grounds), how excited they all were about their new stadium, and how the Withdean is so cold that one match a few years ago many Millwall fans left at half-time. I said I didn't see any Posh fans leaving and we were two-nil down. I think we can now safely assume Posh fans are harder than Millwall fans. That's a fact right there.

The second half kicked off and Posh came out with real purpose. Unfortunately purpose doesn't stop centre-halves being skinned for pace, and after Brighton's Wood had done Langmead and pulled the ball back, it was 3-0. Not quite the beginning any of us had been hoping for. On came Wesolowski and Posh went at it once more. We began to get on top and after Mackail-Smith crossed for Tomlin to head in, the home crowd were anxious. Then Boyd twisted and turned outside the box before lofting a shot onto the underside of the crossbar. It was our last chance and the game ended 3-1.

When the final whistle blew we applauded the players and Fergie off and vacated the ground. On the walk back to the bus stop, unusually, I was full of positives. We talked about how we'd had probably the best team in the division on the ropes for 40 minutes, and wondered how many opposing teams had caused the sort of anxiety amongst the home fans that Posh had for the last 10 minutes. Next week was another game, we agreed, and we would win that.

After a short walk we reached where the buses were supposed to be. Instead all we saw was a line of people stretching as far as the eye could see. "That's not the queue for our bus." My dad decided. So we walked the entire length of the line which by time we finished felt like we were half way home. "Is this the queue for the park and ride bus?" we enquired. "Yeah" said the only bloke in a yellow jacket anywhere in sight, with half an iPod falling out of his ear. So back we trudged, incredulous at the failings of Brighton's matchday public transport systems, while also slightly impressed at the orderliness of its inhabitants (it really was a very long queue).

Once the walk of shame to the back of the queue was complete we huddled in the freezing cold and my dad decided to indulge in his favourite past time, shouting complaints about things to people who have absolutely no control over them. Usually call centre operators or Belgium train conductors, on this occasion it was an unsuspecting Brighton fan second from last in the queue. The poor sod. "Is this how it normally is?!" was the opening salvo, followed quickly by "You can't put some bloody buses on?!? You've got a football game on and no buses!?!!!" The unfortunate gentleman tried explaining that it was probably due to the fact that the trains weren't running. A foolish mistake, he was talking to a man who hasn't listened to reason since 1974. "Well they should put on more buses then, shouldn't they!?!!" The bloke begrudgingly agreed before I intervened to explain that this bloke presumably had nothing to do with the situation. He was a good sport to be fair.

It turned out the park and ride was only a five minute drive and we could have walked back quicker! But never mind it was warm inside and soon we were at the car. I wished the accosted man all the best for the rest of the season, he did the same. We really are quite civil at heart, us football fans.

Finally we were at the car, back in the warm and homewards bound. We had seen a defeat, but a good performance. As far as beginnings go it was inauspicious but maybe, we thought, it was the beginning of something beautiful.

Chris Chapman.

* * * * *

22/01/11

Peterborough United 4 - 0 Hartlepool

Mackail-Smith '62
Rowe '66
Tomlin '68
Wesolowski '90

Posh: *Lewis, Whelpdale, Kennedy, Langmead, Bennett, Rowe, Wesolowski, Lee, Mackail-Smith, Tomlin, Boyd. Unused subs: Collis, Little, Mendez-Laing, Davies, Obika, Clayton, Basey.*
Hartlepool: *Kean, Austin, Humphreys, Liddle, Collins, Horwood, McSweeney, Gamble, Monkhouse, Sweeney, Hartley (sub Bjornsson 53min). Unused subs: Flinders, Boyd, Yantorno, Haslam, Mackay, Murray.*
Attendance: *5,800 (338 Hartlepool fans)*

During the week I found out that I had been given some free tickets thanks to nPower, so I was really up for this game. It was also the first home game since the rather remarkable return of Darren Ferguson, which added a bit more excitement to it.

So, come 5:30am, I was up, and packing my stuff ready to catch the 6:20am train from Leeds down to Peterborough (I don't recommend this… Leeds station at 6am is a horrible place). After arriving in Peterborough I got a bus over to Yaxley to say hello to my family, since I hadn't seen them since Christmas, then off to town to meet my friends.

We did our usual routine, Ladbrokes then Charters to get some pre-match pints. I was hoping my bold ambition of predicting 7 draws on my bet would pay off big. I also had a cheeky punt on CMS first scorer at 9/2. I only stuck £3 on it though.

Charters was packed with Posh fans and a few Hartlepool fans scattered around. I got talking to one of them, who insisted the return of Ferguson had done nothing but play in to their hands, and that they would walk away with a comfortable victory. He mentioned something about some record about not conceding much on the road, but I wasn't worried. London Road would be bouncing, Fergie's homecoming made sure of that.

After walking down to London Road, I had to do a quick stop at the collection point and collect the tickets given by nPower. It's only when I got these that I realised they were in the main stand and not the LRE, which I was rather gutted about, but never mind. I gave the spare to my mate who didn't have a ticket and we took our very uncomfortable seats in the main stand.

It was my friends first game in a while, and she was commenting on how big Lee Tomlin was for a footballer. She then insisted that we, and everyone around us, called him Tubby for the rest of the match. Everytime CMS went through on goal I stood up with my first scorer bet in hand, willing it in. The two lads in front found it hilarious and ended up hoping CMS scored first too! He missed one or two in what was a dull first half, but one mainly dominated by us!

Half time came and I needed to stand up purely because the wooden benches in the Main Stand had made my bum feel so numb it was terrible. Bear in mind I'm also 6 foot 4 and the leg room in the Main Stand is about as big as George Boyd's barber bill. Me and my friend discussed the first half, she was impressed with Tubby and CMS, and was hoping that the second half was better.

The second-half started and Posh stayed in control without creating too much. Hartlepool had very few efforts and Posh were just waiting for the right opening for them to break the deadlock. Ferguson was screaming at the players from the touchline, urging them to be patient but keep attacking.

He was right to do so, as Wesolowski headed a ball across the box, and Mackail-Smith headed in to to give Posh the lead, and me a little return on my bet. We had barely stopped celebrating when Tomlin found Boyd whose shot was deflected on to the bar by the Hartlepool keeper only for Tommy Rowe to follow up and double the advantage. Cue a smile from Fergie.

Then four minutes on from that we had added another as Mackail-Smith showed why he is the ultimate striker. He broke down the wing, and delivered a superb cross for Tubby to head home. My friend was understandably overjoyed that her new favourite had bagged a goal. Hartlepool did have one decent effort as a long range effort from what must have been about 40 yards caught Joe Lewis off guard and hit the post, but Posh were comfortably in control now and enjoying the football, and most importantly, playing like a team again. Something you could see Fergie was delighted about.

We got a fourth in the last few minutes as the ball came to James Wesolowski in the box and he finished neatly putting a very nice gloss on the score line.

After the game, we met up with my friends in Chartlers (they stuck to the terrace rather than the Main Stand, and I can't blame them. I don't think I've ever sat in a more uncomfortable seat in my life) and discussed the game. We all agreed Charlie Lee deserved the man of the match award, and that maybe, just maybe, bringing Fergie back was the correct decision going on that performance.

I went in to Ladbrokes to check on my 7 game draw bet, unfortunately, I managed to get zero out of seven right, but I did collect the cash that Mackail-Smith had earnt me, thus moving him higher in my estimations - if that is even possible.

Then I headed home to get a lovely home cooked meal before setting off on the horrible journey back to Leeds, with a smile, thanks to Posh.

Conor King

* * * * *

28/01/11

Colchester United 2 - 1 Peterborough United

Gillespie '37 Rowe '1
Mooney '86

Colchester: *Williams, Beevers, Clarke, Izzet, Bond, Perkins, Gillespie (sub Odejyai 70min), Mooney (sub White 88min), Coker, James (sub Wordsworth 70min), Heath. Unused subs: Cousins, Vincent, Henderson, Vilhjalmsson.*
Posh: *Lewis, Kennedy, Langmead, Lee, Wesolowski (sub Frecklington 87min), Boyd, Mackail-Smith, Rowe (sub Mendez-Laing 84min), Bennett, Whelpdale, Tomlin. Unused subs: Little, Davies, Nana, Collis, Basey.*
Attendance: *4,645 (375 Posh fans)*

In the games I have been to this season I have seen Posh score 85 goals.

Tommy Rowe's first minute header at Colchester was not one of them.

I can't attend as many away games as I'd like to but several weeks ahead I'd put a few quid by and booked the day off work, as had my travelling firm which consisted of my girlfriend, Tara and our mate Pete. Buoyed by the return of Fergie & the possibility that 'If we win at Col U, I can see us winning the league by 6 points' (Paul Donnelly) along with the fact that Colchester 'had a nice little ground now' (Brianposh) I was really looking forward to this one.

We set off at 4pm for this Friday night game and comfortably avoided the potential A14 /M11 snarl up, arriving at our chosen pub at about 5.30 where we learnt Lesson #1, which was this – Don't trust internet pub reviews. 'A wide selection of local ales and hearty home cooked food' in reality meant 'Greene King IPA and massively overpriced sausage, egg & chips. So, swift half downed and a couple of miles later we turned up at another, somewhat uninviting looking pub which turned out to have a great range of beers and I learnt Lesson#2 which was - Don't ever volunteer to be the driver. It also had a brilliant menu which was cheap and the portion sizes were massive.

An hour successfully killed with a few other Posh fans and we headed off to the ground with plenty of time to spare, especially as I'd had the foresight to do a bit of research and prepay £6 for a parking space. A small navigational error aside, we got off junction 28 of the A12 and...........stopped dead. Traffic was backed up as far as I could see and by the time we crawled to the front of the queue there were only five minutes until kick off. Still, all I had to do was confidently wave my nice yellow pass at a friendly local bobby and we'd sail through the hold up and be in our seats in time for the whistle.

"Good evening officer, I've got a prepaid car park pass."

"Sorry mate, car park's full."

"But I've got a prepaid car park pass."

"The club have told us that no-one else can get into the car park, you'll have to park at Escape."

"Oh, what's Escape?"

"Dunno, I've just been told to tell people to go there."

"Where is it?"

"Dunno, now move along sir, there's a queue here."

"But I've got a...."

Long story short, we parked up on a verge about half a mile away and started running to the ground which isn't easy with half a stone of calamari and spicy potato wedges in your belly. We passed a couple of other latecomers who informed us that "We're 1 down already" Great I thought, not only are we going to miss half of this bloody game but we're already losing. It didn't occur to me at the time that we may be mistaken for people from Essex and it wasn't until we got into the ground, having run through a half empty car park (Aaaaarrrggghhh!) and the solitary open turnstile that we found out that, in fact, we were 1-0 up.

"Best goal I've ever seen & you missed it."

Lesson #3 – Don't believe Adi Mowles.

Having got my bearings, Lesson #4 swiftly followed – Don't

believe Brianposh. The Weston Homes Community Stadium is not 'a nice little ground'. It's a soulless plastic dump on the edge of a bombsite on the outskirts of town.

As for the rest of the game, Posh dominated but were guilty of trying to arsenal the ball into the net - arsenal: verb – to overcomplicate matters when just sticking your foot through the bloody ball would probably be the best option. A couple of defensive howlers later, notably Kelvin Langmead deciding that 4 inches off the ground was a sensible height to attempt a clearing header and we're 2 – 1 down. Neither Whelpdale's deft chip against the post nor Charlie Lee's thunderous crossbar shaker could redeem matters. James Wesolowski's comedy dive was a brave but ultimately fruitless effort to try and nick something and there you go, the best team lost.

It was clear that Fergie's new fangled diamond midfield wasn't the answer to our defensive frailties and the simple fact was that we had just three points from his three games since returning. This season was going nowhere.

A cold walk back to the car and a long tedious drive home followed by an angry e-mail to Colchester United regarding the parking balls-up completed the evening. Well almost…

A quick look at londonroad.net revealed that - "CMS was really starting to piss me off, he's pointless without a proper strike partner. It really does amaze me after watching that that he's one of the league's top scorers." (c. Bendtner 52)

Lesson #5 – Have faith.

Ralph White

* * * * *

February 2011

01/02/11

Peterborough United 5 - 3 Sheffield Wednesday

Mackail-Smith '16, '90	Johnson '5
Boyd '26, '74	Madine '21
Mendez-Laing '84	Sedgwick '35

Posh: *Lewis, Kennedy, Langmead, Lee, Wesolowski (sub Little 46min), Boyd, Mackail-Smith, Rowe (sub McCann 61min), Bennett, Whelpdale (sub Mendez-Laing 67min), Tomlin. Unused subs: Jones, Frecklington, Davies, Basey.*
Sheffield Wednesday: *Weaver, Buxton, Morrison, Reynolds, Coke, Potter, R. Johnson, J. Johnson (sub Teale 46min), Sedgewick (sub Jones 80min), Madine, Mellor (sub O'Connor 73min). Unused subs: Jamesson, Heffernan, Beevers, C. Morrison.*
Attendance: *6,480 (1,384 Wednesday fans)*

There are some days that no matter what you do, everything will go wrong, and to top it all off I just had a feeling that Posh would crash at home to Sheffield Wednesday. The day started badly, and little did I know but it was about to get a whole lot worse. But I was going to Posh tonight, and with Ferguson back in charge, the good times were now surely just around the corner.

After fighting off issue after issue and crisis after crisis at work that morning- which did take my mind off whether we would play the diamond formation again, and who would play at the bottom of it – the clock struck two and I faced the 170 mile journey up to Peterborough. It was all planned, plenty of time to get there, brief trip to say hello to the relatives, get parked, wander into town for some dinner, and then off to London Road. Easy.

Far from it.

The first setback was Basingstoke. A setback for most people at the best of times, so commiserations to those that live there, but I became snarled up in the most horrendous of traffic jams leading to the M3 being closed northbound. So I went through Basingstoke and picked up the A34 at Newbury. Problem solved.

Problem solved apart from the accident on said road. Tempers fraying slightly, detour number two started and I picked up the M4 at Chieveley heading towards the M25 at Heathrow. By now it was rush hour and I crawled along the M4 for what seemed like forever, finally reaching the M25 about two and half hours in. 73 miles done in two and a half hours. Great start, and thoughts briefly crept in about turning around but I carried on, positive that the journey would get better.

Wrong.

Next problem was the eternal road works at Watford, which somebody kindly decided to have an accident in, snarling up the traffic even more. Closer to Peterborough now than home I continued, with the now vain hope of getting there before kick-off. But then again I hadn't bargained for Stevenage. Now I understand that a lot of people work there and commute but I still can't fathom as to why there were monumental queues to get into that shithole at 6pm, unless George Boyd was making a personal appearance at his old club - in which case I'd have joined the masses to touch him.

Starting to question my sanity and whether I'd ever get to London Road, I finally approached the outskirts of Peterborough just after 7pm, but predictably got stuck on the slip road off the Nene Parkway. Finding somewhere to park would be the easy bit of the trip, Ebs always being a safe bet, apart from this Tuesday night. Instead I headed towards the fairground car park on Oundle Road, knowing that I'd have to pay an overinflated amount and be stuck there until midnight after the final whistle. So only five and a half hours after the journey had begun, I had arrived, no pleasantries to family, no dinner, several detours but at least I would get to see Posh.

This had to be worth it; surely the night couldn't get any worse? The day had started off badly, the journey up was abysmal and within five minutes Jermaine Johnson, Wednesday's pacy winger had torn Whelpdale a new one and Posh were 1-0 down. Thoughts already turned to getting back in the car and heading home.

But I stayed and my faith was restored just ten minutes later. A great run and shot by Lee Tomlin fell straight into the path of CMS who inevitably equalised from close range. Wednesday however, were up for this and proceed to lay siege on the Posh goal. Sedgewick missed a presentable one-on-one minutes before Gary Madine benefitted from a Langmead deflected clearance to make it 2-1. Car keys were reached for.

George had obviously made it out of Stevenage alright, and equalised with a shot that their keeper made a right mess of. 2-2 and only 25 minutes gone, maybe this was worth it after all. A further ten minutes later and it wasn't. Poor old Whelps was being given a horrible time by Johnson and was left exposed by Wesolowski again, for Wednesday to utilise the acres of space on the right hand side to make it 3-2.

So to get a half time cuppa…only to be greeted by another queue. Ah f**k it.

Luckily for Whelps, Wesolowski was replaced by Little at half time, who himself had been pretty hopeless for most of the season and Whelps was restored to a more familiar midfield role.

That helped Posh immeasurably, as well as the inevitable bollocking they undoubtedly all received, and they began to dominate proceedings, absolutely destroying Wednesday for the entire second half. Firstly super George equalised with a clever finish and London Road was bouncing, we all knew there was only one winner now. The game changing moment came midway through the second half as CMS's constant tormenting was finally too much for the Owls defence and they resorted to the only option they had – hacking him down when clean through. Wednesday down to ten, and it was matter of when and not if for the next Posh goal.

Recent crowd favourite Mendez-Laing - although all that seems to take these days is a good cross against Swindon - replaced the beleaguered Whelps and Posh went in for the kill. Five minutes from time the Midlands Nandos muncher eventually converted from Tomlin's superb ball and the roof came off the London Road End. The fog rolled in and the pleasure was all Mackail-Smith's as he ran the length of the field to make it 5-3, slotting into an empty net.

So eight goals, a welcome three points and from a personal perspective, a Posh goal for every hour that it had taken me to get there. All worth it, and now for the relaxed drive back. I'd be home in just under three hours and all would be well with the world. But then there was the car park, and that fog I mentioned…

I finally got home at 3.30am, having not being able to see more than 15 yards in front of my bonnet for the entire journey, and sat in a f★★king queue on every stretch of motorway I went on. By now it may have been late, but Posh's run to the play-offs was being timed to perfection.

Chris Dowsett

* * * * *

05/02/11

Peterborough United 4 - 4 Southampton

Mackail-Smith '39	Chaplow 13
Whelpdale '45	Lambert (pens) '31, '47
McCann (pen) '55	Hammond '50
Tomlin (pen) '90	

Posh: *Lewis, Little, Kennedy, Langmead, Lee, Boyd, McCann (sub Ball 87min), Mackail-Smith, Bennett, Whelpdale (sub Mendez-Laing 70min), Tomlin. Unused subs: Jones, Wesolowski, Rowe, Davies, Basey.*

Southampton: *Davis, Harding (sub Dickson 65min), Fonte, Lambert, Barnard (sub Forte 85min), Do Prado (sub Richardson 75min), Butterfield, Hammond, Seabourne, Oxlade-Chamberlain, Chaplow. Unused subs: Bialkowski, Jaidi, Gobern, N'Guessan.*
Attendance: *6,905 (1,287 Southampton fans)*

For those with a nervous disposition you may wish to look away now, or skip ahead to Charlton away.

Sky have decided that this will be their Saturday evening game, which you have to say was an inspired call on their part. Posh's record of scoring and conceding make us 'the great entertainers' of the Football League and Southampton have continued their ascent of the League 1 table. Let us not forget that just two seasons ago Sky were covering Saints in the Premiership and both sides have excellent young prospects in their squads. The stage was set for us to showcase League 1 at its best, during primetime Saturday evening. Lights, camera, action. We did not disappoint.

We set off mid afternoon and with a nod to a former PUFC chairman dined at Pizza Express. Sam and George quickly demolish the set menu for kids before heading to London Road, dodging the Saturday shoppers and as boys will be boys, just had to climb as many pieces of street furniture that can be found along the way. Bridge Street becomes an improvised assault course.

Taking our seats in the Upper Glebe I texted a pre-kick off photo to a Saints fan watching on Sky. Christopher replies saying: "cracking picture, the pitch looks good". Truth is the surface is suffering badly from the winter and I fear that Gary Johnsons' 13mm optimum grass length standards may now be slipping. Slowly the appearance of the grass around the centre circle is taking on an unnatural resemblance to that of Wayne Rooney's hairline, pre the implants.

The game commences and as anticipated in an open, attack minded fashion, both sides have chances to open their account. Deadlock was broken on 19 minutes when Barnard's fierce shot was blocked by Lewis and a static Posh defence looked on as Richard Chaplow darted through to poke the ball home. Fergie had no doubt warned the defence about Chaplow having been at Preston under DF, it would appear our defence weren't listening.

Both sides kept each other keepers busy, however things got harder for Posh when Mark Little needlessly chopped down the pacey Alex Oxlade-Chamberlain as he pressed into our box. Penalty to Saints, duly converted by Rickie Lambert. The next goal would be crucial.

Some nerves were creeping in to Posh, and rushed shots kept being taken when more often a better opportunity may have come from a pass. Posh got themselves back in the game when Tom Kennedy headed to Boyd, who flicked to Tomlin, who lofted the ball for a charging CMS to show his strength in slotting the ball under Davis whilst battling off a defender. At the close of the first-half it was back to all square when Grant McCann sent in a glorious cross for Chris Whelpdale to again demonstrate his heading prowess and make it 2-2.

Right then, second half all to play for. The game does not let up and CMS just shots wide after Tomlin again played him on with a well timed ball. Saints then march up to the London Road End and Kennedy rather harshly is judged to of fouled that man Chaplow, again in the penalty area. Lambert steps up to calmly help himself to his second penalty goal, 3-2 to Saints.

It's still end to end and Posh have a penalty claim rejected when Fonte pushes Tomlin, a tempting proposition for most opposition players I acknowledge, but injury is then added to insult when on 50 mins Saints regain their two goal advantage as a slick corner routine feeds the ball to Hammond who takes his chance well. 4-2 to Saints, another hill to climb.

Saints appear to think that having regained a two goal lead that's it, for normal teams psychologically it probably would be. But Posh back once again under Fergie's guidance though do not crumble, do not shirk, just keep going. We're pressing hard and Kelvin Langmead of all people bursts into Southampton's box causing uncertainty, if not panic, and not just for Southampton. Seaborne prematurely ends Langers up-field excursion, with a clumsy challenge, a penalty is finally awarded to Posh. Grant McCann does not waste the opportunity. 4-3 to Saints, with 25 mins to go the game is there for the taking. Mendez-Laing replaces Whelpdale, and he is deployed to run at the Saints, and again this causes more concern and uncertainty for the Saints defence.

Saints are wasting time at every given opportunity as the pressure is increasing from Posh. Davis, called into frequent service, stretches taking goal kicks beyond any measure of reasonableness. As we end the second-half the siege of Southampton's goal is relentless. Five minutes of extra time is awarded mostly for Davis' antics. Players are crammed into Saints area and NML's shot is handled by the hapless Seaborne. McCann is now on the bench so it falls for Lee Tomlin to take the spot kick and restore parity. 4-4 the final score and four the number of penalties.

So another defining game, in a season of defining games. Twice a two-goal deficit was restored against a quality side such as Southampton. It says a hell of a lot about the new spirit in the camp, contrast and compare this attitude to the one we took in November to St Marys for a spanking. Some of you would pay good money for that I know … but it is this inner belief, dogged determination and the sense of disappointment that we hadn't won this game that will get us promoted.

16 goals in two games, wow.

Chris Sharpe, St Albans

* * * * *

12/02/11

Charlton Athletic 3 - 2 Peterborough United

Charlton Athletic	Peterborough United
Jackson '57	Tomlin '29
Wright-Phillips '59	Mackail-Smith '90
Langmead (og) '80	

Charlton: *Elliott, Dailly, Doherty, Bassone (sub Fry 62min), Wagstaff (sub Abbott 46min), Francis, Jackson, Semedo, McCormack, Eccleston, Wright-Phillips (sub Reid 80min). Unused subs: Worner, Racon, Reid, Fortune, Jenkinson.*
Posh: *Lewis, Little, Langmead, Bennett, Kennedy (sub McCann 85min), Rowe (sub Ball 76min), Whelpdale (sub Mendez-Laing 59min), Lee, Boyd, Tomlin, Mackail-Smith. Unused subs: Jones, Wesolowski, Davies, Basey.*
Attendance: *15,909 (1,017 Posh fans)*

Darren Ferguson made the surprise choice of bringing Tommy Rowe back into the starting line-up to replace Grant McCann. The formation, however, remained the same as Posh continued to use the diamond as their formation of choice. Chris Powell's appointment at Charlton has given The Addicks a renewed hope of promotion and they went into this game full of confidence, having won all three of Powell's previous games in-charge.

The hosts were quick to put Posh under pressure creating a succession of corners in but it was Posh who had the first chance of note. Lee Tomlin collected the ball on the half-way line as Peterborough looked to mount a swift counter attack and he quickly set about showing the skill that has excited the Posh fans so much this season. A clever nutmeg of Alan McCormack allowed Tomlin to run straight at the Charlton defence and he cleverly slotted a pass into Chris Whelpdale who failed to capitalise on a good opportunity dragging his shot wide of the far post.

It would have been the perfect start for the visitors who often start games slowly but even with the missed opportunity Darren Ferguson's men were dominating proceedings. Short, sharp passing and clever movement from the attacking trio of Craig

Mackail-Smith, Lee Tomlin and George Boyd was causing the visitors no end of problems and if it wasn't for Rob Elliot's awareness in goal Posh may have created some more early chances.

As the half progressed Posh continued to look the better side. Retaining possession well and looking dangerous in an attacking sense with the side continuing to make good use of the width of the pitch, bringing both full-backs into play on regular occasions. It seemed inevitable that they would create some more chances if they continued to attack in this manner. After capitalising on a sloppy pass from Johnnie Jackson Tomlin had a chance to run at Federico Bessone before smashing a shot on goal which was turned onto the inside of the post by Elliot with the ball bouncing clear.

Posh had hardly given Charlton a sniff so far but the hosts did produce a nice move to give Eccleston some space in the area but Joe Lewis was alert in the Peterborough goal, hurrying off his line to deny the chance.

Lee Tomlin had looked the best player on the pitch so far. His combination of skill and knowledge of the game is rarely found at this level and it seemed that Darren Ferguson had spotted this, with the manager giving Tomlin license to roam in the attacking positions. When the former Rushden player did pick up the ball it seemed he had it in a fairly innocuous position, out on the left flank, but a clever run saw him get to edge of the Charlton box before cutting inside, putting the ball between Jose Semedo's legs, and curling a perfectly placed finish into the top corner of Elliot's goal to give Posh a deserved lead.

Just as the visitors had gained some real momentum their progress was halted by a bizarre stoppage. Referee Mr. Webb went down in some pain seemingly under no contact and the stretcher had to be called for before he was replaced by fourth official Mr. Stewart. It had been the worst time for the stoppage to occur with Charlton now having a chance to regroup after the set-back, indeed it had been the first goal they had conceded since Powell's appointment. However, Posh continued to press, even after the length stoppage, and a Tom Kennedy free-kick could only be pushed away by Elliot in the Charlton goal as the visitors looked to extend their advantage before the half-time whistle.

As the first half was brought to a close Posh would have been very happy with their display. It had been their best 45 minutes away from home and they had been the far superior team and should have already been out of sight. Charlton could have had few complaints if they were further behind but Posh had not been ruthless enough in front of goal and the hosts were still in with a chance at 1-0. That said if Posh could maintain this standard of performance for 90 minutes it would be an uphill struggle for Charlton to get anything out of the game.

At the break Chris Powell chose to change his attack bringing Pawel Abbott on to replace Scott Wagstaff. Many teams would have sat back on their advantage but not Posh. Immediately they went in search of an elusive second goal, pushing men forward in numbers. The attacking mentality almost paid off too. After a good pass from Tom Kennedy, Lee Tomlin was released, this time down the right hand side of the pitch, and he drilled a great cross into the box which sat perfectly for Craig Mackail-Smith to head into an empty net. Or so it would have seemed. Yet somehow, Mackail-Smith, who has been in scintillating form in recent weeks, didn't manage to make meaningful contact and the glorious opportunity went begging.

Posh continued the early onslaught and Mackail-Smith went close again before George Boyd's shot from the edge of the area was well held by Elliot. For a team with Posh's defensive record 1-0 is not a safe position. And the numerous chances that Peterborough had failed to capitalise on were making the large contingent of away fans nervous – you can only afford to miss so many of these opportunities before you are made to pay.

And all of a sudden Posh were. Simon Francis, who burst forward from right-back, put in a delicate cross to the far post for Johnnie Jackson to head home. It had been a hammer blow for Posh. Charlton's first chance of any note had given them the lead and all of a sudden The Valley had sprung to life.

The goal had provided the spark that the hosts had needed. Red shirts were piling forward and the pressure soon became too much for Peterborough. After some slick build-up play Nathan Eccleston put in a similar cross to the one that had led to the first goal, spotting Posh's weakness, and Wright-Phillips unmarked at the far post headed home. The striker had been quiet so far but it was this sort of composure in-front of goal that makes him one of the top marksmen in League One.

Posh had gone from seemingly having three points in the bag to having to fight back from behind and it seemed that could no longer string a pass together. All of a sudden the patient attacking play of Posh had turned into aimless hoof-ball, reminiscent of the Gary Johnson era.

Charlton almost added a third as Abbott and Wright-Phillips both went close but Lewis stood firm in the Peterborough goal. Ferguson realised that his team were on the verge of collapsing and replaced Chris Whelpdale with the spritely Nathaniel Mendez-Laing

The substitution had worked and Mendez-Laing was providing an outlet ball for a Peterborough team that had lost their composure. Three times he rounded his marker before shooting, twice, and pulling the ball back once but Boyd inexplicable stepped-over the ball seemingly thinking someone was better placed behind him to take the shot on. Indeed, the substitute should have gained Posh a penalty, when he was clearly tripped inside the area, but the referee signalled that the foul had occurred outside the box.

It wasn't long before the match was put beyond doubt either. Awful defending again allowed a succession of crosses to be put into the box. Charlie Lee's clearing header only reached Pawel Abbott who lashed home a deflected volley from the edge of the area.

Posh don't know when to give up though and when six minutes of injury time were shown it seemed to provide hope to their ambitions of snatching something from the match. Storming forward they began to put pressure on the Charlton defence and Mark Little whipped over a cross to Mackail-Smith who smashed home a volley from close range. It was a good finish but if he had taken his chance at the start of the half as well as this one it may have been a far more meaningful one.

As the final whistle blew Posh fans left The Valley stunned. Posh had completely dominated proceedings but the hosts had proved more clinical. Once again we were let down by a defence that can't defend. If we had a competent defence we would cruising to the league title now.

Of course, some of the blame must lie with Ferguson but he has inherited the problems of the Johnson regime. Kelvin Langmead continues to look a division out of his depth, in my opinion, and Mark Little needs time to develop. Gabriel Zakuani's return cannot come soon enough.

Although results, and the position in the table, suggest differently there has been a dramatic improvement in performances since Fergie's appointment. We could, and perhaps should, have had seven points from three tough away fixtures but were not clinical enough, and did not defend well enough, to take them. This has to be worked on. But gone are the days of hopeless, aimless, long balls and we are now playing slick passing football that suits our attacking talents.

I honestly believe it will not be long before we go on a lengthy unbeaten run, the fixtures become easier on paper for a while now, and we must capitalise. We are on the verge of something special here at Posh, I can feel it, and when it finally clicks, which I believe it will, we will go on a run. Whether this run takes is into the automatic places is debatable. Southampton, Charlton and Brighton are a long way ahead of us now. But will we make the playoffs? I'm almost certain we will.

John Verrall

* * * * *

15/02/11

Yeovil Town 0 - 2 Peterborough Utd

Mackail-Smith '85
Basey '88

Yeovil: *Henderson, Huntingdon, Smith, A. Williams, Ayling, S. Williams (sub Russell 76min), Johnson (sub German 84min), Ehmer, Upson (sub Virgo 87min), Tutte, Wotton. Unused subs: Martin, Alcock, Calver, Gibson.*
Posh: *Lewis, Little, Zakuani, Bennett, Basey, Rowe (sub McCann 60min), Wesolowski (sub Mendez-Laing 63min), Lee, Tomlin (sub Ball 83min), Boyd, Mackail-Smith. Unused subs: Langmead, Kennedy, Davies, Jones.*
Attendance: *3,351 (154 Posh fans)*

Living in Devon means, by necessity, we have to travel for work and for the past 10 years has meant the daily trip across the Somerset border to the delights -not- of Yeovil. The first six years working at a well known helicopter manufacturer in town have seen me suffer constant jibes about the greatness of Yeovil Town and how poor Posh were – to be honest it was difficult to disagree! However, this all changed four years ago but in a one off game anything can happen. Remember how they did us at London Rd two seasons ago? So I looked forward to the game with a certain amount of trepidation.

This was a re-arranged fixture taking place on a cold Tuesday night in February, not one for the armchair fan but despite this I decided to pop up to Huish Park a few days before the game to purchase a couple of tickets. Why? They were two quid cheaper and I am not one to pass up a bargain even though I knew no more than a couple of hundred die hards from Peterborough would be travelling down.

Unfortunately my boy was unable to attend the game and with no way of getting rid of the ticket I resigned myself to going on my own. Surprise, surprise my better half (Sarah) agreed to come along. This was really something as she last attended a Posh game way back in the early 1980's. We were living in Middlesbrough at the time so Hartlepool it was. The only reason she came to that game was because she planned to spend time in Hartlepool shopping but took one look at the place and said: "no way, I will suffer the match."

After 30 odd years I thought the delights of Yeovil Town FC might not be enough, so to show how grateful I was I decided a treat was required so off we went for a romantic pre-match meal of fish and chips at Palmers chippy; a well known Yeovil establishment. A quick pre-match tour of the Huish Park subbuteo stadium stuck out on a business park did nothing to excite her so we retired to the "marquee" which serves as the bar area. To be fair there was a nice atmosphere inside with both sets of fans mixing freely. The highlight had to be meeting BrianPosh plus a few others from londonroad.net and also the infamous BrizzlePosh.

The game was not really much to write home about and the first half passed by relatively quietly. Posh were playing reasonably but while Yeovil had lots of possession they carried very little threat. It was good to see Zak back after injury and, although he possibly lacked the edge and match fitness, we looked comfortable at the back. Half-time 0–0. Spent the break chatting to a few Yeovillites from work who of course said that they were not impressed with Posh. I said we just needed one chance to fall to CMS and he would bury it.

The second-half continued in much the same vein and as the match approached the last quarter the temperatures dropped sharply and most were looking forward to getting warmed up in the car or coach on the trip home. A bore draw looked the likely outcome. But suddenly from nothing up popped the great man himself – CMS had his chance and put it away. 1 – 0 Posh. We were getting warmed up now and began to make some noise and a few minutes before the end a corner from Posh ended up bouncing around in the Yeovil area and up steps Count Bassey to smash it home from 6 yards. 2–0 Posh. Game over.

Yeovillites began exiting faster than an elephant's bottom after a vindaloo as Posh played out the rest of the game with no problems. Not a spectacle by any means, but we just needed to grind out the results to keep us on course for the promotion bid. Job done by Fergie and the team.

A stroll back to the car and 30 minutes later we were sitting at home, fire on and hot chocolate to hand. Did Sarah enjoy the game – it was OK was the reply. A quick look at the pictures on theposh.com the next day caught Sarah smiling and clapping at the end – maybe it will not be another 30 years before she attends again. To round it all off I childishly spent the next week parking next to anyone in the works car park displaying a YTFC sticker making sure my "Proud to be Posh" sticker was in full view.

John Middleton

* * * * *

19/2/2011

Peterborough United 2 - 1 Tranmere Rovers

McCann '53 Welsh '24
Showunmi (og) '70

Posh: *Lewis, Little, Zakuani, Lee, Boyd (sub Rowe 85min), McCann, Mackail-Smith, Bennett, Mendez-Laing (sub Ball 65min), Tomlin, Basey. Unused subs: Jones, Kennedy, Langmead, Wesolowski, Davies.*
Tranmere: *Warner, Cresswell, Goodison, McChrystal, Showunmi, Welsh, Taylor (sub Weir 75min), Kay, Labadie, Akins (sub Bakayogo 65min), Elford-Alliyu. Unused subs: Collister, Cathalina, Robinson, Wood, McGurk.*
Attendance: *5,774 (233 Tranmere fans)*

If you were going to attend just one game of Peterborough United's 2010-2011 campaign, a cold, wet February afternoon at home to Tranmere Rovers would probably not be at the top of your list. However, that turned out to be the only game I managed to attend this season.

Prior to this season I had been a season ticket holder for over 25 years. However, after only being able to attend a handful of games in the 2009/10 Championship season due to increasing family commitments I reluctantly decided not to renew my season ticket, and resigned myself to getting my weekly Posh fix via the Statler and Waldorf of the airwaves - namely Edwin Overland and Bob Burrows at Radio Cambridgeshire.

It wasn't until five days before the game, Valentines Day, that I knew I would be going. My partner had bought me a pair of Mr Men novelty socks as a gift with Mr Perfect on them - presumably the Mr Grumpy ones had sold out. As I opened them I felt that there was a piece of card inside one of them. Initially I thought it was a lottery scratch card, giving me the opportunity to win £1,000s which she would then no doubt spend on my behalf. However, when I removed it I discovered a ticket for Posh v Tranmere the following Saturday. Who said romance is dead?

In the week running up to the match, the National press were reporting London Road as being the UK's premier entertainment venue. You get more bang for your buck at Peterborough with an almost guaranteed 5 goals per game. I immediately texted a friend to warn him that "I'll be at the game on Saturday so expect our first 0– 0 draw since December 2009.

Finally Friday evening arrives, and I start to make mental plans for my pre-match activities until I hear: "those doors we need are 20% off at B&Q. As you're going to Peterborough tomorrow you could get them before the match?" and with that my plan for a pre-match pint at Eb's was foiled.

The following morning I was wondering whether there would be a match at all given the overnight downpour. However, as Sky Sports News had no news of a postponement I set off for Peterborough anyway. After all those doors aren't going to buy themselves.

At B&Q I remembered that Craig Mackail-Smith used to

work at a similar store whilst playing non-league football so I scouted for any potential replacements. Unfortunately, none of the staff appear to fit the young and hungry criteria, although Joan on the tills' blue rinse would be a big hit on the terraces.

Once inside the ground I took the opportunity to view the very impressive Posh kit history painted on the walls of the concourse before taking up what used to be my usual seat in the upper tier of the Glebe. I'm heartened to see that all the same old familiar faces are still there, albeit with hair a little greyer after enduring the previous 18 months following Posh.

Having not attended London Road during the Gannon or Johnson eras - or should that be errors? - I jokingly ask the bloke behind me if I'd missed anything whilst I'd been away? "You ain't missed a thing!" came his response.

Truth is though, I have missed it. When ex-professionals are asked what they miss most about the game, they nearly always say the same thing -the dressing room banter. It's the same with being a fan. It's not necessarily seeing the actual matches you miss. Live radio commentary, BBC's "Football League" programme, BBC website, PUTV, SKY, the ET etc all combine to make sure you can probably see more Posh action now without actually attending than you ever could before.

What's you miss though is sitting or standing shoulder-to-shoulder with fellow Posh fans and experiencing it together. You miss the terrace witticisms, the atmosphere, the conversations, the laughs, the friendships. Internet forums, such as London Road.net, and the new Standing on the Glebe podcast go a little way to recreating this, but the actual experience can never be replaced.

And so to the match. I can't remember many Posh v Tranmere games being overly spectacular affairs and this game wasn't any different. The pitch was sodden from the overnight downpour, and cut up pretty easily. Surely, Tommy Robson couldn't be describing it as "much better than the pitches I used to play on" as he nearly always does when co-

commentator on Radio Cambs.

It was Tranmere who adapted to the conditions the better in the first half, with their large powerful striker Enoch Showunmi looking the danger man as they worked the channels well. Showunmi pounced on a horrendous Ryan Bennett error and laid the ball across for John Welsh to slot home from the edge of the area.

Starved of the ball in midfield, Grant McCann started to drift out of position trying to get involved in almost every Posh move meaning the team lost any semblance of shape. Furthermore Ferguson's decision to play Mendez-Laing from the start appeared only to enhance the player's reputation as an impact player coming on from the subs bench. But Posh have come back from far worse scores than 1-0 down at half time this season.

In the second half, McCann became more influential and within 10 minutes of the restart he'd levelled the scores with a bit of a bobbler in to the bottom corner from the edge of the area. Keen to keep the tempo up, Boyd raced to retrieve the ball from the back of the net. Tranmere's keeper Tony Warner, a man personally challenged in the follicle department, tried to prevent George from doing this by pulling him back by his flowing black locks and snapping his hair band in the process. Of course, none of this was witnessed by the referee or linesmen.

As he had threatened in the first half, Tranmere's Showunmi popped up with the match winner - a bullet header at the near post. Luckily, he was trying to defend a Posh corner brilliantly delivered by McCann. And that's how it finished. 2-1, and another three points, to the Posh.

It's often said that it is these sort of games that get you promoted. Winning ugly. And although the final whistle was not greeted with a rendition of Status Quo's "Rockin' all over the World" at least I can say:I WAS THERE.

Sean Ingham, Bourne

* * * * *

22/02/11

Peterborough United 1 - 1 Colchester United

Boyd '6 Henderson '17

Posh: *Lewis, Little, Zakuani, Bennett, Basey, Boyd, Wesolowski (sub Mendez-Laing 46min), McCann, Tomlin (sub Ball 75min), Lee, Mackail-Smith. Subs: Jones, Kennedy, Langmead, Rowe, Davies.*
Colchester: *Williams, Clarke, Izzet, Perkins (sub Wordsworth 60min), Coker, White, James (sub Bond 89min), Heath, Odejayi (sub Vincent 89min), Henderson, Mooney. Subs: Cousins, Powell, Beevers, Vilhjalmsson.*
Attendance: *5,758 (279 Colchester fans)*

Darren Ferguson had hinted that he would have made changes to his team at the weekend had he known that the pitch was so poor so it wasn't too surprising to see James Wesolowski return to the starting line-up, dropping into central midfield, at the expense of Nathaniel Mendez-Laing. The change provided Posh with more 'bite' in the midfield whilst Lee Tomlin returned to his favoured position up-front. John Ward's Colchester side had struggled on the road of late but he named the same starting eleven as he had for the previous two games.

The atmosphere at London Road was subdued from the off. A succession of big fixtures in terms of the promotion race, against Southampton, Charlton and Sheffield Wednesday had been focused on far more than fixtures against Colchester United and Tranmere United, both with outside chances of making the play-offs, rightly or wrongly, and the mood reflected this. The game started quickly though with both teams missing early chances. The visitors went close first when Lloyd James was gifted too much time to get a shot off but Joe Lewis palmed the ball away. Posh countered almost instantly when Craig Mackail-Smith checked inside his marker before curling a shot which Ben Williams, in the Colchester United goal, could only parry back into the path of George Boyd but he couldn't generate enough power on his shot to give Posh the lead.

Posh who would make the first telling break-through of the match though when Lee Tomlin and Boyd exchanged passes outside the box before the latter lashed home a powerful drive into the back of the net. Posh had momentum now and were quick to look for the chance to extend their advantage. Lewis sensed the chance to counter as he launched a long-throw to Mark Little who was flying forward at pace and when the full-back slotted a pass back inside for Tomlin who curled a shot against the outside of the post.

Despite the lead Posh had been nowhere near their best. Struggling to find a player in a blue shirt and panicking defensively the performance had, at times, been reminiscent of that produced far too often under Gary Johnson. Colchester's direct approach was evidently causing problems as Kayode Odejayi's physicality was proving hard to deal with. It wasn't long before the visitors capitalised on Posh's defensive weaknesses either. A relatively innocuous cross was not dealt with properly by the Peterborough defence and Ian Henderson was granted far too much space to float the ball over Lewis' head and into the top corner. It was Colchester's first away goal in over 500 minutes of away football.

Posh then had a goal chalked off when Craig Mackail-Smith was flagged offside after he poked the ball over the line after Lee Tomlin had been brave to win a header from Nathan Clarke. The striker seemed convinced that he had made his run from an on-side position and was quick to tell the referee's assistant just that. However, it was the visitors who looked the more likely scorers of the third goal and Clarke and Odejayi were guilty of missing opportunities as the visitors bombarded Posh with long-throws and a succession of set-pieces.

As the first half neared its conclusion Mackail-Smith created a chance for himself but William's acrobatically tipped the shot over the bar before Grant Basey poked a volley wide. It was evident that something wasn't quite right for Posh. The side looked fatigued but more worryingly bad habits from the Johnson era had been evident: too many hopeful balls had been hit forward and every time the ball went near the Peterborough box panic seemed to set in. Credit had to also go to John Ward who had certainly done his homework on Posh. He was leaving Henderson out wide to capitalise on the weaknesses of Ferguson's favoured diamond formation, and time after time he had been free to run at an exposed Grant Basey. Ward had also told his midfield to defend deep, sitting just in-front of the back-four, to minimise the space for players like Lee Tomlin and George Boyd to roam and cause problems in.

Ferguson had realised his system hadn't worked to the desired effect too. Mendez-Laing was brought on to add more attacking impetus and to utilise his pace, given the open nature of the match. James Wesolowski was the man to be replaced as Ferguson noticed the need for a little more craft and guile in his attack.

Both 'keepers were called into action early on in the second-half from long-range efforts but neither was tested too heavily as clear-cut-chances remained hard to create. Even though the game was end to end Posh still looked disjointed and weren't replicating some of the slick build up that has been displayed under Ferguson so far. In-fact it was the visitors who were again looking the more likely to score especially from the direct attacking routes they had available to them such was the physicality they possessed in their side. Nathan Clarke's long throw had created chaos all night and Ben Coker almost capitalised when he unleashed a volley at Lewis who did well to parry the shot.

The London Road crowd were becoming restless. Urged to go forward by their supporters Posh seemed intent on slowing the game down and playing countless number of passes along the back four. And these nerves from the crowd seemed to affect the players too as Posh continued to struggle. Restlessness almost turned to anger soon later though. David

Mooney was inexplicably allowed to burst through both Posh midfield and defence to get on the end of a basic long-ball from Nathan Clarke and as he bore down on Lewis' goal somehow Ryan Bennett charged back to make an inch perfect tackle to deny Mooney a definite goal. Bennett's error against Tranmere at the weekend had been inexcusable but it was defending like this which has drawn top level club's interest to the young centre back.

Charlie Lee almost provided Posh with an underserved lead when he powered a header just wide of goal from a Grant McCann corner. But the visitors were quick to continue to the pressure they had been exerting on the Posh defence. A succession of shots were fired on Posh's goal but bodies were being thrown in-front of the efforts as Peterborough tried to avoid falling behind.

As the minutes ticked away Posh simply weren't looking like scoring. Boyd had a chance but his touch was heavy and he couldn't make room for the shot. Mendez-Laing continued to charge and charge at the Colchester defence but his final ball was poor on countless occasions. In-fact Colchester almost snatched a late winner, as they did when the two teams met at the Weston Homes Community Stadium, when Ian Henderson smashed a shot from long-range it seemed that Lewis would make a comfortable save but he slipped at a crucial moment before adjusting brilliantly to tip the shot wide of the post.

As the fourth official indicated there would only be three minutes of added time Posh were becoming desperate. The game needed a moment of magic. After watching his team try and fail for most the match Mackail-Smith decided to take matters into his own hands. Collecting the ball on the half-way line the jet-heeled striker set off, sprinting past two Colchester defenders before smashing an effort on goal but Ben Williams did wonderfully well to tip the ball out for a corner.

It had been a frustrating evening for Posh. In terms of the

table we did not fall any further behind the automatic places as results elsewhere went our way but to make automatic promotion you must capitalise when others slip up. It is no good simply matching others now; we must better them. The play-offs seem our most likely way of gaining promotion – too much time has been wasted playing mediocre football under Johnson. What this draw has done is turned Oldham into a game that is now a must win if we harbour ambitions of automatic promotion. A loss there would be disastrous and would even begin to make us look nervously over our shoulders at teams below us.

However, we have had three tough fixtures where we have had to dig-deep in a week and have achieved 7 points. That, in any context, is not disastrous in a league where teams continue to show their vulnerability and slip up on a regular basis. The performance was not sparkling and was arguably our worst since Ferguson returned but we still managed to get a point against a decent outfit in Colchester. Promotion remains the aim and despite this set-back we are still reasonably well-placed.

John Verrall

* * * * *

26/02/11

Oldham Athletic 0 - 5 Peterborough United

Rowe '49
Ball '52
Zakuani '61
Mackail-Smith '68, '83

Oldham: *Amos, Todd, Mantram, Taylor (sub Reid 69min), Lee, Morais, Stephens, Evina, White (sub Jones 75min), Tounkara (sub Brooke 58min), Trotman. Unused subs: Brill, Feeney, Tarkowski, Black.*

Posh: *Lewis, Little, Kennedy, Zakuani, Lee (sub Wesolowski 90min), Ball (sub Mendez-Laing 73min), Boyd, McCann, Mackail-Smith, Rowe (sub Davies 86min), Bennett. Unused subs: Langmead, Whelpdale, Basey.*
Attendance: *4,263 (412 Posh fans)*

Boundary Park. Oldham. Last time here was two years ago in another successful league one campaign and the result that day summed up the season for me. 1-1 coming into the last few minutes until CMS hassled the centre half, forced an error and finished it off. I knew we were going up after that game, so today's game had high standards to meet.

Results prior to this game were hit and miss, but both performance and confidence had generally been raised since Fergie's glorious return. Oldham going into this game were considered to be strong competitors for a play-off place, and despite recent financial difficulties were without doubt tricky opposition.

We were fortunate enough to wangle tickets in the directors box through a very good friend, so three of us sat suited and booted in the warmth of the directors suite and two others joined 410 other hardy Posh fans outside at the 'Coldest Ground In The Country'. We rocked up around 12.30 and having been greeted by both Oldham and Posh Chief Execs we duly tucked into some cracking Meat and Potato Pie. Chatting through all matters football, Oldham and Posh - including some interesting insights into an ex Posh loanee now with Oldham - time was quickly progressing and kick off was nearly upon us.

Nevertheless, there was still time for our DoF to arrive, along with Ricky Hatton, his latest champion protégé complete with belt, and a full blown camera crew recording all shenanigans. It was at this point we looked at each other in complete agreement - this was without doubt the most surreal football experience we'd had yet.

The game kicked off and we were looking confident from the off. Boydie had a Premiership quality move that ended with him shooting inches wide after just a few minutes and I thought if we continued like this it would only be a matter of time before we were ahead. CMS wasted a one-on-one and Zak steered an unmarked header incredibly off target. As the half wore on we started to leave gaps at the back, which resulted in an opportunity for Oldham that really should've seen us concede. Nevertheless, the first half was pretty even - we looked comfortable without getting out of first gear, whilst Oldham seemed relatively short of ideas. At 0-0 though you can never tell and at that point the next goal could have been the winner for either side.

The second-half of this game was however completely different to the first, and a totally one sided affair that saw us play some truly majestic football. Old school Boydie was back and his performance in this half was one of the best I had seen for a long time, with his movement, creativity and range of passing making him absolutely unplayable. And he was being supported by a team all performing to perfection, and our previous problems retaining the ball non existent.

0 - 1: Slick approach play between Boyd and Ball, ending with Rowe expertly directing a shot into the far corner past the keeper.

0 - 2: A brilliantly worked free kick from McCann, headed back from Rowe and nodded in by Ball.

0 - 3: Zak ghosted in unmarked heading in another McCann corner and suddenly we were set piece experts.

0 - 4: Great (albeit deflected) through-ball from McCann allowing CMS another one-on-one that he finished this time around with a deft dink.

0 - 5: And so as there was no doubt, the best was saved to last, a sublime volley from CMS. A free kick from McCann came off the head of Zakuani, found CMS 15 yards out and he sent a thunderous shot past the helpless keeper. What. A. Goal.

We were absolutely brilliant in the second half, and the diamond formation couldn't have worked better. Special mention must go to Ryan Bennett too who I thought was absolutely superb.

Sitting with the Oldham Directors for this game they didn't expect to see us again next season, and clearly nor did a number of their fans who rose to their feet and applauded CMS' scorching volley.

This was a fantastic day and game for us all, and left me full of confidence that we would give this campaign a bloody good go, and if we didn't make it we were going to be very close and do ourselves damn proud in the process. Not enough superlatives were there to describe how well we played and it was yet another day when we could be honoured to be Posh fans.

We were also moving into March, and all Posh fans know our recent history under Fergie at this stage of the season. There were some further big tests coming up in the next few games, starting off with the home game against Exeter, could we keep the run going and build on this performance?

Ashley Hepper, Padiham, Lancashire

* * * * *

March 2011

05/03/11

Peterborough United 3 - 0 Exeter City

Boyd '10, '74
Mackail-Smith '87

Posh: *Lewis, Little, Kennedy (sub Wesolowski 76min), Zakuani, Bennett, Boyd, McCann, Rowe, Lee (sub Davies 88min), Mackail-Smith, Ball (sub Tomlin 59min). Unused subs: Jones, Mendez-Laing, Langmead, Basey.*
Exeter: *Hamer, Tully, Duffy, Henville, Taylor, Harley, Noble (sub Dunne 84min), Nardiello (sub Logan 65min), Golbourne, Cureton, Sercombe. Unused subs: Krysiak, Cozic Stewart, Jones, O'Flynn.*
Attendance: *6,174 (357 Exeter fans)*

I was chosen to be mascot for the Peterborough United v Exeter City game.

I went to the ground with my Mum, Dad and Hannah my sister. My Nan and Grandad came along later to watch the game. At the ground, I met Steve from the Free Kicks Foundation and Simon who looks after the mascots.

I was given the kit and got changed. I went to the dressing room to meet the players and get autographs. I had my picture taken with Joe Lewis, Craig Mackail-Smith, Tommy Rowe and George Boyd. I had a tour of the ground. I then went out onto the pitch for a training session. Just before kick off I lead the team out with two other mascots. I walked out with George Boyd.

The game kicked off and Peterborough played well. George Boyd scored on 10 minutes. It did get a deflection on one of the Exeter's defenders. Mark Little was unlucky not to score a few minutes later. At half-time it was 1–0.

After half time, Lee Tomlin came on and nearly scored. On 74 minutes Craig Mackail-Smith ran into the box, passed the ball to George Boyd who scored his second. A few minutes from time George Boyd passed the ball to Craig Mackail-Smith and he scored.

It was a fantastic day and I will never forget it.

Aidan Brooks.

* * * * *

08/03/11

Notts County 0 - 1 Peterborough United

Lee

Notts County: *Nelson, Darby, Edwards, Lee, Ravenhill (sub Sproule 54min), Bishop, McDonald, Gow, Westcarr (sub Brandy 71min), Harley, Demba-Nyren. Unused subs: Burch, Clifford, Thompson, Chilvers, Sodje.*
Posh: *Lewis, Little, Kennedy, Zakuani, Lee, Boyd, McCann (sub Langmead 90min), Mackail-Smith, Rowe, Bennett, Tomlin (sub Ball 75min). Unused subs: Jones, Wesolowski, Mendez-Laing, Davis, Basey.*
Attendance: *5,714 (1,412 Posh fans)*

After setting off from work early to meet up with a group of friend we set off on the relatively short journey to County. Hampered by roadworks on the normal route the driver insisted he knew a short cut. From this particular individual this is usually bad news as previous short cuts have resulted in situations from being hopelessly lost to once managing to turn up at the wrong football ground. After the longest short cut I have been on in some time and the usually hour-long journey taking nearly double that we arrived. A deft move on his part then ensured a parking space near the exit of the market car park way ahead of our turn.

On approaching the six open turnstyles, the two older members of our group went through their designated entry point. We however were greeted with a queue of about 30 people all waiting to get into the same turnstyle. Rather unbelievably County only had one open for adult admission with no pre-bought tickets. We joined the queue and after a couple of minutes of not moving anywhere started to moan about the time it was taking to get in. A steward wandered over to, I thought at the time, remind me to keep patient, etc , etc. Instead he asked me how many we were expecting to bring tonight. I explained that with a few wins and the Fergie Factor along with a chance of still getting automatic promotion probably between 1500 and 2000. He then asked if I was f***ing joking and got on his radio to his Superior. We couldn't quite hear the conversation but the steward became more and more agitated as it progressed. The radio was put away and he returned to tell us that they had been briefed not to expect any more than about 300 fans. He then shuffled off to either do something proactive or more than likely swap positions with a colleague so he didn't have to deal with the hassle.

The game itself was a drab affair really. Posh fans were still coming into the ground about half-an-hour after kick off and more and more of the seating was being opened up. The first-half passed without major incident, bearing in mind the last time these teams faced each other the game finished in a cowboy style mass brawl on the pitch at the end of the game.

The second half was more of the same until Charlie Lee decided he'd had enough and ran a full thirty yards with the ball before smashing it into the net from distance. Lewis performed an excellent save towards the end to ensure we took all the points from the game and that was that. The Fergie Factor was in full effect and discussion on the way home - using a different short cut of course - was all about whether we could do it or not.

Rhys Thrower

* * * * *

12/03/11

Peterborough United 6 - 0 Carlisle United

Rowe '2
Mackail-Smith '24
Boyd '45, '83
Bennett '77
Ball '90

Posh: *Lewis, Little, Kennedy, Zakuani, Lee (sub Davies 69min), Boyd, McCann, Rowe (sub Mendez-Laing 71min), Bennett, Tomlin, Mackail-Smith (sub Ball 69 min). Unused subs: Jones, Langmead, Wesolowski, Basey.*
Carlisle: *Collin, Simek, Murphy, Robson, Taiwo, Zoko (sub Madden 58min), Marshall (sub Wells 90min), Curran, Berrett, Cooper, Arter (sub Loy 70min) Unused subs: Caig, Thirlwell, Loy, Swinglehurst.*
Attendance: *6,467 (385 Carlisle fans)*

My introduction to Posh shortly after moving to the area was an extremely cold 0-0 against Plymouth in January 1997. At that time, and after that performance, I didn't expect some 14 years later to be an avid supporter and dedicated season ticket holder. It was the vision of DMac that ignited my support for the club and that meant that I've now held my seat in the Glebe for the last four seasons.

DMac's young and hungry transfer policy along with Ferguson's dedication to attacking football means come Friday morning prior to a home game I get as excited as a child before Christmas. Even the disaster of the 2009-2010 season in the Championship failed to dampen the excitement as we aim to bounce back to the second tier of English football.

Quite early on in the 2010-2011 season, under Gary Johnson, I got the feeling that something wasn't quite right and started to worry that the amount of goals we were conceding along with our poor away form would mean that we would remain in League One for the foreseeable future. The global economic situation meant that DMac, quite understandably, was having to spend more time on his business affairs overseas and was missing from the majority of home games and the relationship between him and Johnson was nothing like the close relationship he had with Fergie.

As Brighton started to dominate the league the thoughts I had in the summer - that we were going to run away with the league - started to evaporate and I was certain we were going to be mid-table come the end of the season. That was until I woke up on the morning of 12 January and looked at my Backberry to see a text saying that Johnson had left by mutual consent. By the time I got to work and logged on to londonroad.net people were already saying that Fergie was on his way back. I studied SkyBet for the odds on who would be the next Posh manager and right from the off Fergie was favourite with it being confirmed later on in the day at a press conference.

Memories of the last couple of seasons soon flooded back and instantly I became more confident that we'd get promoted back to the championship. There were people who said Fergie shouldn't come back and that he'd never repeat his previous success but I always felt he was the right man for the job.

Twelve games had passed since Fergie had returned to the club with Posh winning seven of these and drawing two before the visit of Carlisle. Johnson had left Posh in 7th place in the league 10 points behind Brighton. The Fergie factor had taken Posh to 4th place in the league and reduced the deficit slightly to 9 points. Clean sheets had been missing from the first half of the season but instantly Fergie had managed to sort this out. It could have been something to do with signing a proper left back...... who knows?

Carlisle had been on somewhat of a hot streak and had moved up to 8th after some decent results. This was a must win game and promised to be tough - how wrong I was. It took just 80 seconds for Posh to take the lead. Proving he's not just a goalscorer but can also make goals CMS slid the ball across to Tommy Rowe who slotted the ball home. Posh then completely dominated with Tomlin, CMS and Rowe all going close. It wasn't until the 24th minute that we got a second with a goal from CMS that proved if he hadn't made it as a footballer he could easily be a pickpocket as he snuck up behind the Carlisle defender to steal the ball and head it into the back of the net. Posh continued to pressure Carlisle and just before half-time Boyd gave the fans a glimpse of the player we all know by using a bit of jiggery pokery to get past a couple of defenders and put the ball under the keeper.

The fans felt at half-time that the match was going to be a rout and predictions of seven and eight nil were suggested. A few more grounded individuals however reminded people of the Cardiff game the season before (obviously with three goals instead of four and in reverse).

Carlisle came out of the traps quickest at the start of the second-half and it was down to Joe to show us why he's so important with an excellent reflex save. If that had gone in then heads could have dropped but instead the attacking prowess kicked in again. CMS continued to pressure Carlisle's defenders with their only option to foul him in the box and a penalty was awarded. McCann missed the resulting penalty and Posh's bad luck continued with a CMS effort ruled out for offside. Posh did however get a fourth shortly afterwards with some penalty area pinball finally ended when Bennett headed into the back of the net. Six minutes later Boyd made it five with a volley that was deflected on route to goal. Carlisle heads had most definitely dropped by the time Ball made it six as he smashed the ball into the roof of the net.

Posh were awarded their second penalty of the game in stoppage time which led to a bit of handbags between McCann -Captain and penalty taker - and Boyd - on a hat trick. McCann stormed away and Boyd put the ball on the spot only to drag it wide. With six goals, two missed penalties and a goal ruled out for offside it could easily have been 9-0.

Whether it was Carlisle who didn't turn up or Posh who excelled or even a combination of both one thing was for sure, as the fans left we felt invincible. The win had pushed Posh up to third, one point behind Huddersfield with a game in hand. The Fergie effect was in full swing with automatic promotion very much on everyone's mind.

Stuart Gilham, St.Ives

* * * * *

15/03/11

Sheffield Wednesday 1-4 Peterborough United

Sheffield Wednesday	Peterborough United
Heffernan '52	Mackail-Smith '25
	Tomlin '35
	Boyd '41, '81

Sheffield Wednesday: *Weaver, Osbourne, Hinds (sub Potter 74min), Morrison, Reynolds, Miller, Coke, Beevers (sub Jones 10min), Teale, Johnson (sub Heffernan 46min), Madine. Unused subs: O'Donnell, O'Connor, Morrison, Mellor.*
Posh: *Lewis, Little, Kennedy, Zakuani, Lee (sub Basey 86min), Boyd, McCann, Mackail-Smith, Rowe (sub Wesolowski 87min), Bennett, Tomlin (sub Ball 73min). Unused subs: Langmead, Mendez-Laing, Davies, Jones.*
Attendance: *16,014 (638 Posh)*

Posh were possibly in the best form for decades. Fifteen goals without reply in the past four games. Wednesday on the other hand hadn't won at home since December. I'd never been so sure of a Posh victory.

I'd just moved back to Peterborough having spent the past five years at university in Sheffield. One of the downsides of being a teacher is that I can't take the afternoon off work to attend a football match, but there was no way I was going to miss this one.

My housemate from Uni also happened to be a Posh fan, so I'd arranged to meet him at the ground. It was going to be tight getting in to Hillsborough. I would have to get the train to Retford, then another one to Sheffield, then jog to the tram stop in the city centre, and finally get the tram to Leppings Lane, but I should be able to make it with about 20 minutes to spare. No trains running back, so Steve Thorpe of Free Kicks Foundation fame offered to give me a lift back to Peterborough.

I bumped into Steve's wife and son Ashley at Peterborough station so joined them for the journey. Ashley is also a student at my school so I spent most of the journey threatening him with detention whilst he read his Match magazine. Then the news I'd been dreading, my connection at Retford had been cancelled. Thankfully I had the trainline app for my iPhone, so worked out that I could change at Donny and still get to Leppings Lane for 19:34 -as long as I could get the tram from Meadowhall – so all was not lost.

Donny station was deserted; clearly no other Posh fans had been stupid enough to leave it so late. The train to Meadowhall seemed like the slowest train in the world, and it made me wonder why I bothered. I knew I wouldn't get home until gone midnight, and I had a full day at work the next day. The train pulled into Meadowhall a couple of minutes early, and we could see our tram, we would make it on time. Unfortunately as we got closer and closer to the platform, the tram got smaller and smaller, it had left early.

We waited about on the freezing cold platform for what seemed like an hour and got the next tram knowing we would be late. It was lucky that I'd arranged to meet Tim at the ground after all. We ran to the ground and got there about 10 minutes late, I stood about looking for Tim. Then I saw him also running up the stairs. Somehow he'd also managed to arrive late despite working in Hillsborough. Thinking about it, in four attempts, we've never seen kick-off at Sheffield Wednesday.

We took our seats near the front behind the world's largest pillar. It did make things exciting as players would disappear behind the pillar before reappearing somewhere completely different. An incredible pass from Lee Tomlin put CMS through to make it 1-0. Tomlin made it 2-0 with a beautiful (and unnecessary) lob ten minutes later. Five minutes before half time Boyd made it 3-0. Unbelievable.

Most of half time was spent trying to get a decent photo of the electronic score board. Although I'd been convinced Posh would win this one, I'd never thought I would see the day that Posh were 3-0 up at Sheffield Wednesday. The Wednesday fans clearly knew what was coming since only 15,000 or so had bothered to attend.

The second-half started and Wednesday seemed to have perked up a bit. Paul Heffernan pulled one back for them, and a minute later a low cross went across the face of goal just waiting for someone to poke it in. The only thing worse than losing, is throwing away a three goal lead. We'd already done it at home to Swindon, and it wasn't something I wanted to experience again.

Time went agonisingly slowly as Wednesday threw attack after attack at us. But after 80 minutes Boyd was able to wrap up the win thanks to some incredible goalkeeping from Nicky Weaver. Boyd fired a tame shot at goal, and Weaver gently wafted it into the top corner.

A brilliant win that put Posh just a point off automatic with a game in hand. Wednesday on the other hand were edging ever close to the drop zone.

Nick Warrick

* * * * *

21/03/11

MK Dons 1 - 0 Peterborough United

McKenzie '69

MK Dons: *Martin, Lewington, Kouo-Doumbe, Mackenzie, Gleeson, Vine (sub Marsh-Brown 62min), Baldock, Woodards (sub O'Hanlon 90min), Leven, Chadwick (sub Ibehre 77min), Powell. Unused subs: Searle, Stirling, Balanta, Chicksen.*

Posh: *Lewis, Little, Kennedy, Zakuani, Lee (sub Davies 70min), Boyd, McCann, Mackail-Smith, Rowe (sub Mendez-Laing 76min), Bennett, Tomlin (sub Ball 76min). Unused subs: Langmead, Weslowski, Basey, Jones.*
Attendance: *10,019*

Imposters; God, I hate them!

If ever a game showed why the imposters should never have been allowed into the football league this was it. I do not refer to the fact they beat us, to be honest we beat ourselves as we could and should have been three up by half-time then allowed them back into the game. A boo boo by Joe finished us off right at the end and because of the result it is not the game I wish to write about.

Oh no, not that this will come as a surprise to anyone who knows me it is the lack of decent drinking establishments that provokes my ire. The game was live on Sky so instead of the normal 3,500 plus Posh attending it was accepted that there would ‘only’ be 2,000 Posh at best, a number that the Imposters could only dream of taking away for a league game.

With that in mind and knowing the facilities around the ground are non existent we left Peterborough nice and early in an effort to find a decent pub that did food as the option of KKC or Mac100%beefmyarsedonalds did not hold any attraction whatsoever. We got to roundabout city around 4pm and headed at first to the pub named after the only reason Bletchley is on the map, The Enigma. Even at that time it was full of Posh, the average age was about 16, but that obviously hadn’t stopped them being served and by their condition it was Stella that was their drink of choice.

Off we went to another pub reasonably local, The Three Trees, a pub that any PISA member who was present the day we took two coaches there will remember with affection despite a couple of locals getting a slap for having the temerity to try and have a go at one of our group. On reflection it was only Steff but as nature has taken the piss out of him far more than any chav from Bletchley could he did deserve the protection he got.

Anyway along with a lot of shops in the area it was boarded up. This was a very large pub that called itself a community pub. Obviously one that the community didn't support. Off we went again and finally found a pub that announced Open from 11-11 serving fine ales and good home cooked food.

The door creaked as we entered and the locals as one turned their heads so surprised were they that anyone they didn't know had entered their den.

Beers ordered it was up to Nilesh the only thin man that is obssessed with food who took it upon himself to grab one of the menus on the tables. The fare on offer did look as good as the advert outside and orders given to Nilesh we all looked forward to what we were about to receive.

"We don't do food on match days", was the reply.

"kin twatty toy town shithole crap arsed wankstain town," was my response which on reflection was a bit much. One town would have sufficed.

So it was beer and crisps for the next couple of hours then onto the half finished ground which even in that state is too good for the club it hosts. A crap day was finished off by a crap result. Having to put up with a few of the locals taking the piss as we left the stadium made future events even more enjoyable.

If only I could have seen into the future so I would have known that we'd ultimately murder them in the play offs I'd not have been quite so pissed off on the journey home.

Adi Mowles

* * * * *

25/03/11

Bristol Rovers 2 - 2 Peterborough United

Kuffour '6 Anthony (og) '23
Hughes '57 Boyd '53

Bristol Rovers: *Logan, Anthony, Coles, Tunnicliffe, Senda, Pell (sub Lambe 62min), Lines, Campbell, Hughes, Kuffour, Hoskins. Unused subs: Green, Brown, Richards, McCracken, Kalala, Williams.*
Posh: *Lewis, Little, Kennedy, Zakuani, Basey (sub Whelpdale 63min), Lee, Davies, Rowe, Boyd, Mackail-Smith, Tomlin (sub Wesolowski 74min). Unused subs: Jones, Ball, Mendez-Laing, Taylor.*
Attendance: *6,569 (416 Posh fans)*

The day started like any other school day, with my dad travelling to Bristol via London due to a work meeting, and a free breakfast. That very nice Adi Mowles offered to take me to the game. I only had two lessons that day as every other Friday I had a 'study period, where we could go home and 'study. I had special permission from school to leave early.

But just before I was meant to leave someone set off the fire alarm. It was either a test or someone had set it off as a prank. After the fire alarm I had to wait ages to get my bike, as the sheds were locked and I needed to get to my Nan's where I was due to be picked up. Just as I got to my Nan's though I saw Mr Mowles' car driving off. I thought I had missed him. When I got into my Nan's I saw his car pull up again phew! I quickly got changed and we were off to Bristol.

We got there about two hours before kick off and we went to the pub for a drink. The pub was right near the ground and I met up with my Dad and we went into the ground. The open terrace on the touchline was cold and we were hoping that it would be an easy win and another step towards automatic promotion. They scored an early goal through Jo Kuffor after some sloppy defending, before we equalised through an own goal. Then came the stupidest moment of the game Mark Little made a silly challenge after just being booked for breathing on Stuart Campbell, who rolled about like he had just had his leg blown off, and it was a red card for Little and the end of his game.

In the second-half both sides went for the win; then after a moment of magic by Tomlin, Boydy scored just in front of us. My picture was in the programme the next game celebrating the goal. But then Jeff Hughes scored a diving header at the other end. The most frustrating moment of the game had to be when CMS ran through on goal, all on his own, kicked it towards the far corner and it rolled just wide. So all in all a game we should've won but didn't.

Ashley Thorpe

As a Poshie living in London I don't get to as many games as I would like. So when my friend asked me to be his best man I thought this is the perfect opportunity to get a Posh away day in. The wedding was in mid-April so I thought March would be perfect timing for a stag do. So I looked at the away fixtures Notts County on a Tuesday, Sheffield Wednesday on a Tuesday, MK on a Monday and the final fixture of March Bristol Rovers away. Perfect. The only other thing the stag wanted to do was a bit of gambling. So because of the fixture change due to the Wales vs England International, Posh played on the Friday night, so fresh from our day at Newbury racecourse which involved plenty of drinking and gambling we arrived at the Memorial Stadium.

When I volunteered to write my diary about the game I remember thinking who scored? Were there any crucial parts of the game that I would need to include? So I asked a few of the boys and this was the response.

We were drunk.
They scored
We scored (CMS)
We had someone sent off
We scored (Boyd)
They equalised

Which I think about sums the game up perfectly. The rest of the weekend ran smoothly in Bristol.

Steven Shaw

My immediate thoughts right now are ones of panic and having put my size 10s right in it. It's all very well volunteering to write a Match Report but remember fellow Poshies that as you begin to approach the autumn days of your life, amongst a whole list of things that start to go wrong or don't seem to work quite so well, the memory starts to fade. Bristol Rovers away, less than three months ago but it's all a bit of a haze right now. Stay with me, it'll all come back. Trust me, it will come back.

I'd love to big-up some pre-match tale but 'Billy No Mates' me. Lived in Bristol for longer than I care to remember and Posh fans around these parts are rarer than a hen's tooth but hey, still Posh and right now, frigging Proud!

Only my second Posh game of the season but don't you dare call me a part-time supporter. Us out of towners are just as passionate as you regulars but without your support systems – you know, a mate to talk to when all things Posh are heading downward and you need some reassurance. No need to feel sorry for us – things are getting easier. Matchdays are now spent logging on to the internet and listening to Uncle Edwin and if we're really lucky, the wise words of Sir Tommy of Robson. If nothing else a radio commentary allows us to dream and boy when we've got Roy of the Rovers in our team, it's pretty easy.

OK, just got back from what us old farts call a 'comfort break.' Where was I? I remember, Rovers away, final score 2-2. This was the night that despite giving it a real go, deep down we all realised that automatic promotion was no longer on.

The evening started so well. Pre-match entertainment was spent watching a group of grown men attempting to hang up a PISA flag. A bit like watching council workers on the job. You know, one person doing all the work and everyone else offering advice. After five minutes when they were no further forward - but to give them their due at least they had got the damn thing up the right way round by this time. I had more pressing matters to attend to. No, not find the toilet but get my pre-match Cornish Pastie and cup of Bovril – you start to feel the cold at my age. I'm telling you, if ever I was on Mastermind, my specialist subject would be Cornish Pasties and believe me, Rovers' Pasties are Champions League class. Lovely pastry, great soggy filling with plenty of meat. I digress – the match.

Slow out of the blocks, within five minutes we're 1-0 down. Sloppy goal. Ball bobbled around our box and no-one could get in the way of it. However, as the minutes ticked by gradually we start to get back into it. Quick ball to Boydy, smashing cross and expertly headed in ....by one of their defenders. Hey, we'll take it, 1-1.

Thereafter a passage of play that led to Mark Little being sent off seconds before half-time. The first was never a booking; the second harsh but given how things had been proceeding, absolutely bloody inevitable. Big Joe was so incensed he charges into their half to berate the ref. One for the record that - first time I've ever seen him take command of anything outside his six-yard box during a game.

Cracking second-half. 10 vs 11 with Rovers desperately needing points to stave off relegation and us needing the three points to keep us in the running for automatic promotion. End to end but after around 55 minutes slick interplay between CMS and Boydy with Boydy smashing it into the net. Great goal, 2-1, happy days!

Just when I was thinking we can do this - always a bit dangerous when watching Posh- we get overrun in defence and they equalise almost immediately. It then starts to go from bad to worse as an almighty balls up between the Count and Big Zak almost leads to them scoring another.

Fergie had seen enough. Basey was hoiked off immediately and in my mind to be discarded into the long grass, Whelpdale like, and forgotten forever. Bearing in mind subsequent events during the play-offs, ain't it amazing how players can go from zero to hero?

OK, hang on. A couple of minutes to go and cue Roy of the Rovers. The ball breaks to Boydy. Brilliant through ball to CMS and mayhem in the Rovers defence. Three defenders chasing him down but he's away. Just outside the box, he steadies himself, then shoots. An exocet missile skimming along the ground and one of those moments when you're just waiting for the ball to hit the back of the net and ....GOAL! Sorry Poshies, not this time. Agonisingly inches, inches, wide. Final score 2-2.

And I suppose that's where my story ends but since you've stuck with me this far, I know you're a dreamer like me so indulge me with a little postscript. It was only a point but in the scheme of things, it was another point that helped us into the play-offs. Against all the odds, we did it. With the help of Roy of the Rovers, my daydreams came true. We really did it! God bless you CMS and thanks for the memories.

Mark Beales, Bristol

* * * * *

April 2011

01/04/11

Peterborough United 3 - 3 AFC Bournemouth

Mackail-Smith '11, '42 — Ings '35
Rowe '15 — Fletcher '71
Smith '90

Posh: *Lewis, Kennedy, Zakuani, Lee, Wesolowski (sub Davies 84min), Boyd, McCann, Mackail-Smith, Rowe, Bennett, Tomlin (sub Ball 88min). Unused subs: Jones, Langmead, Whelpdale, Mendez-Laing, Basey.*
Bournemouth: *Jalal, Cooper, Pearce, Pugh (sub Fletcher 52min), Robinson, Feeney, Smith, Wiggins, Hollands (sub Arter 87min), McDermott, Ings (sub Lovell 73min). Unused subs: Stewart, Purches, Partington, Dalla Valle.*
Attendance: *6,670 (275 Bournemouth fans)*

For the second time in less than a fortnight, Posh played in front of the Sky cameras and Joe Lewis provided the armchair fans with another display which made some question if his bright future was in danger of becoming a thing of the past.

Posh tore into the match and were two up within the first 15 minutes. After a barren streak of two whole matches, Craig Mackail-Smith restored the natural order with a classy finish on 11 minutes. He took a superb pass from Grant McCann on his chest before firing neatly inside Shwan Jalal's left post. Tommy Rowe followed this up four minutes later with a net bursting strike after a penetrating run from midfield.

The hosts dominated for the next 15 minutes but Bournemouth gradually made their presence felt. From a corner, Joe Lewis called to punch away an in-swinging ball but misjudged its flight, leaving Danny Ings to tap the ball in at the far post.

Bournemouth continued their pressure but Posh forced a corner just before half time, which Ryan Bennett flicked on for Mackail-Smith to shin home. It was a far more convincing contact than Pat Gavin made for most of his Posh goals, but CMS owed a lot to the beleaguered Jalal expecting a bit more meat behind the effort.

So with the two goal lead restored and Bournemouth's rally vanquished, it looked plain sailing for Posh to secure the three points and give their automatic promotion aspirations a touch of reality. Unfortunately, the next 45 minutes would give them a hefty brush of realism.

Again, Posh established a high tempo but Lee Tomlin and Mackail-Smith couldn't add to the lead despite chances falling to them. Bournemouth elected to bring on the aging Steve Fletcher on 52 minutes. Fletcher has been to London Road more often than your typical council official so it was no surprise that Bournemouth adopted a more direct approach. The question was whether Fletcher still had the brawn to match his proven nous. It turns out that he had.

After withstanding a lengthy Posh mauling which featured a rare save by Jalal from a George Boyd shot, a harmless looking cross from Warren Feeney was watched by the whole of London Road as it floated lazily to Joe Lewis's far post. Lewis figured that the defence would deal with it whilst they wondered how something so slow could stay in the air for so long. They probably considered the same about Fletcher as he rose in installments over the gazing defenders to head the ball in to the net via the unprotected far stick.

Buoyed by their breakthrough, Bournemouth continued to belt high balls into Posh's penalty area with Fletcher and defender Jason Pearce alarmingly coming frequently on top during the bombardment. Stoppage time arrived and Fletcher was showing no signs of flagging as he headed wide but it seemed that Posh had done enough to secure all the points as the defence cleared what appeared to be Bournemouth's final salvo. However, the midfield lost the ball and Bournemouth made their way back to Posh's penalty area, with a swift exchange of passes. A block from Bennett seemed to have thwarted the danger and Adam Smith's goal-bound prod didn't look like it should trouble Lewis. But it would. The ball found its way beneath Lewis's midriff and the only sound in the whole ground was the 200-odd Bournemouth fans celebrating an unlikely equaliser.

All other areas of the stadium were simply stunned. Posh had done more than enough to win this match but errors had proven costly. The recent run which had engendered so much optimism had petered out into a frustrating sequence of two draws and defeat from three matches. Furthermore, Posh's lack of success against teams in the top six was becoming a widely held concern. If we couldn't beat them during the bog-standard season, how would we fare against one or two of them in the play offs? What had seemed an inexorable march was facing a worrying deviation.

Paul Myland

* * * * *

05/4/11

Dagenham & Redbridge 0 - 2 Peterboro' United
Ball '3, '8

Dagenham: *Roberts, McCrory, Doe, Arber, Green (sub Currie 83min), Akinde (sub Scannell 81min), Nurse, Ogogo, Vincelot, Gain, Lee. Unused subs: Lewington, Antwi, Savage, Currie, Bingham, Lancaster.*
Posh: *Lewis, Little, Kennedy, Zakuani, Lee, Wesolowski (sub Langmead 90min), Ball, Boyd, McCann, Mackail-Smith, Rowe. Unused subs: Jones, Whelpdale, Mendez-Laing, Davies, Tomlin.*
Attendance: *2,063 (405 Posh fans)*

If you ever thought Peterborough was grim.....don't go to Dagenham for a day out. After we beat D&R in the League 2 promotion season, we spent the hour long tube journey back into civilisation saying we hoped we would never have to go back to that ground. Dagenham just about qualifies as London in so many ways.

Dirty Dicks at Liverpool St Station is the venue for the pre-match drinks after having decided we wanted to be in and out of Dagenham in less than two hours (including the game). Pre-match at D&R is improved slightly now that for some reason they have given the away fans the new, very well kitted out stand behind the goal. I even managed to sneak a beer back to my seat and supped away whilst watching the game, when a steward spotted me he just chuckled and shook his head.

Unlike others that have forgiven him and see his work at D&R as brilliant, I don't like John Still. His time at London Road produced football that was grey, lukewarm and lumpy and I always want to batter teams he manages for that very reason.

Here we are on a Tuesday night with rain in the air, tiny ground, smaller crowd and against a team fighting for it's League 1 life. In the old days, this would be a scenario that Posh would bottle. Under Fergie MkII things are very different.

After four minutes we take the lead through the impressive David Ball, after eight minutes he scores again. Against a decent side, Posh being two goals to the good would worry me but against D&R it's time to settle down for the next 82 minutes safe in the knowledge that three points is coming our way.

The next 82 minutes is honestly the most boring spell of football match that I have ever watched, enlivened only by D&R keeper Tony Roberts reactions to the crowd and Gaby playing the 'how far can I head the ball game.' I spent the time daydreaming that I would hopefully never have to come back to this ground again. I write this three days after Old Trafford, with a smile on my face, hoping beyond hope that we never have to go back.

Jamie Jones

* * * * *

09/04/11

Huddersfield Town 1 - 1 Peterborough United

Hunt '90 McCann (pen) '41

Huddersfield: *Bennett, Peltier, McCombe, Clarke, Naysmith, Roberts, Ward (sub Gudjonsson 46min, sub Hunt 78min)), Arfield, Kilbane, Rhodes (sub Novak 62min), Afobe. Unused subs: Colgan, Morrison, Lee, Cadamarteri, Hunt.*
Posh: *Lewis, Basey, Zakuani, Bennett, Lee, Rowe (sub Mendez-Laing 82min), McCann (sub Davies 78min), Wesolowski, Boyd, Ball (sub Whelpdale 87min), Mackail-Smith: Unused subs: Langmead, Frecklington, Tomlin, Jones.*
Attendance: *16,431 (1,246 Posh fans)*

I've often wondered for a footballer what the low point of a career may be? Relegation? Career threatening injury? Being released from a club? A five year old picking your goalkeeping performance apart? If it's the latter clearly Joe Lewis reached the nadir of his career prior to the Huddersfield game.

I attended the Bournemouth game with my son Harrison - 5 years old going on 50 - the previous week. During that game we had raced into a 3-1 lead only for Big Joe to play his part in blowing the game. Frankly, it may not have been all Joe's fault but for the next week over breakfast and dinner I constantly heard how Joe had one of those silly games and had given away our points. Normally it is pretty easy to zone out Harrison at times if he becomes obsessed with something, unfortunately once Oliver, his four year old brother picks up on it also the task becomes harder. Therefore at times in lovely stereo and surround sound I have Harrison repeatedly talking about Joe having a silly game and then Oliver asking why did Joe have a silly game? Once or twice is fine but when every other sentence is about Joe or why did Joe do this or that . .arghhhhhh!

To solve this and seek some respite I decided/demanded that we go to Huddersfield to banish the memory and give them something else to talk about. My Dad joined us for the trip also and on Saturday morning we set off from Coventry.

After reaching the end of the M69 and joining the M1 Oliver had fallen asleep and Harrison was in full Joe mode again "I hope Joe doesn't have a silly game again." This time the conversation was with Dad and the turning up of the radio meant I only needed to smile and nod in the rear-view mirror as Harrison presumably talked through each of the goals that were Joe's fault complete with arm and hand movements indicating how Joe could have done better.

We approached Huddersfield after exiting off the M1. The abiding memory I have is of those walls made of different stones that appear in every northern rural area you go to and second the phenomenal amount of speed cameras that lined one main road into Huddersfield. Says a lot for Huddersfield that the main memory of the town is speed cameras.

After finding parking close to the ground and paying some man who looked more like a nightclub bouncer with impossibly large arms - perhaps he was one of the 'I'll look after your car for a couple of quid mister' kids that grew up into a car park attendant - we sat in his shitty car park eating our sandwiches and talk turned to the game. We simply had to win -at least that's what I remember thinking - to keep up our hopes of second place, something which had seemed impossible until the return of Darren Ferguson. Little did I realise at the time that come the end of the season this game would die and fade to the back of the memory thanks to an infinitely more important and pivotal match in Manchester against the same opponents.

We walked to a pub on a corner full of Posh and Hudders fans. Whilst keeping the lads occupied outside as Dad headed to the bar I ended up chatting to a couple of other Poshies who had been staying in Huddersfield for the weekend. We all spoke about the need for a Posh win and how absolutely forgettable the away game at Dagenham & Redbridge - sandwiched between Bournemouth and this game - had been.

On reaching the away end of an admittedly impressive

stadium it suddenly dawned on me that I had no cash for the turnstiles. I then needed to make a dash down some ridiculously steep set of steps (why can't everywhere be as flat as the fens?) to the cash point where I had the good fortune to stand behind Mr and Mrs Huddersifeld. 5Ft 2 and decked out in full kit and flag regalia, and both full of mouth about how easy the game was going to be and how they owed us one for '92 - they were never old enough to have been alive for that game, a quick check of Mrs Huddersfeld's bum fluff on her chin confirmed this.

No game against Huddersfield is complete without mention of that famous night almost twenty years ago. Unfortunately I didn't get to see that game as, one I was tucked up in bed sleeping waiting for school the next day and secondly I had no passion for Posh or desire to support them as I hated football. That is until my dad and his mate took me to Wembley for my first game and I've been hooked ever since (although admittedly my dedication waned in the early to mid 2000's thanks in part to living in Southampton and god awful football under the stewardship of everyone's favourite pantomime villain).

One thing that struck me after I'd climbed the steps back up to the stand, was that we had brought a fair few and also the atmosphere was building into something special. This improved the more we gained control of the game and there was only ever one team in it, although Huddersfield did threaten occasionally as - I think - a Ryan Bennett clearance off the line demonstrated. Despite being outnumbered (not for the last time against Hudders) we out sang (definitely not for the last time against Hudders) them and this only increased when McCann slotted his penalty home with typical aplomb.

Half-time and Harrison gives his usual insightful summing up of the game "definitely a penalty dad" and "Joe is still being a bit funny isn't he?", something which I felt was a bit harsh but you can't tell a five year old anything.

The second-half started, such was our control Huddersfield

had no chance of getting anything from the game. We were in complete control, the songs were being sung and the atmosphere was the best I could remember in many a long time. Unfortunately Posh did start to lose their grip of the game and had to cling on as at times they were outplayed. Then deathly silence as a penalty is awarded to Huddersfield. It's fine I say to myself we've got Big Joe on hand. I look at Harrison shaking his head but I had full confidence in Joe. So much so I couldn't look.

At the time I remember thinking we're throwing away second place, our season is in disarray, we're falling apart at the seams. . . .then the almighty roar but from our end. What happened? what happened I asked to no one in particular and Dad informed me Joe had pulled off a save. You beauty Joe!

Harrison was jumping up and down shouting for Joe, (he's always loved Joe and was now definitely his best player). Unfortunately as you learn with Posh at times we don't always follow the rules and disappointment looms. This time disappointment was in the form of Jack Hunt, surely a euphemism if ever there was one? Hunt absolutely started to murder Basey with his direct running at him, and Basey, left with no cover from his teammates was being made to look poor and every inch the Barnet player he had once been.

Surely Ferguson would notice this and replace Basey or give him some help? But no. As the clock ticked down the Huddersfield fans erupted. Jack Hunt had equalised.

"What did that man say", Harrison asked as somebody shouted at the Huddersfield fans. Luckily thanks to the name I could easily tell Harrison the man was simply saying "you, Hunt" trying to get Jack's attention. I prayed during the remaining few minutes of the games, firstly that Posh could hold on and secondly that Harrison wouldn't call Oliver a Jack Hunt in the garden in front of their mother or at any time at school, otherwise their trips to the football would surely be over.

The game ended in a draw and extended Huddersfield's

unbeaten run. On the way out I put Oliver on my shoulders as a squat bald Huddersfield fan started to mouth off at a Posh fan. Usually bald headed nutcases demand your respect however when this one started speaking he was more Joe Pasqaule than Calzaghe and the moment passed however his one sentence stuck with me: "You were f★★king shite we'll always kill you over two legs' obviously forgetting the game in 92 and demonstrating the arrogance that 35,000 Believe t-shirt wearing fans would take to a whole new level come May.

I turned to Harrison as we walked to the car: "wasn't it good dad? Lewis saved a penalty, not everyone can do that can they? I knew he wouldn't have one of his silly games'. This was a delight to hear the first time. After a two hour trip home I was ready to take him to the next game in the hope that someone else could provide a talking point! Oliver had his first experience of an away game and loved every second, mainly because he got to play with his toy car on the back of the seat in front of him at the ground but everyone has to start following Posh somewhere!

Pete Berridge

* * * * *

16/04/11

Peterborough United 2 - 1 Plymouth Argyle

Bennett '55 Fletcher '38
Mackail-Smith '70

***Posh**: Lewis, Little, Lee, Zakuani, Bennett, Boyd, McCann, Wesolowski (sub Frecklington 63min), Ball (sub Davies 78min), Mackail-Smith, Rowe (sub Tomlin 46min). Unused subs: Jones, Taylor, Langmead, Whelpdale.*
***Plymouth:** Button, Duguid, Fletcher (sub Summerfield 71min), Arnason, Fallon, Bolasie, Peterlin (sub Mason 86min), Walton (sub Patterson 79min), Paterson, Nelson, Zubar. Unused subs: Larrieu, Timar, Young.*
***Attendance:** 6,723 (492 Plymouth fans)*

Joe Lewis overcame recent inquisitions into his faltering form to spectacularly secure a much needed win from this dour encounter against League 2 bound Plymouth. It certainly wasn't a match for the purist and but for Lewis's display would soon have been forgotten amongst a season of exceptional scorelines.

Plymouth came to London Road in the depths of administration and knowing that their recently imposed ten-point deduction had doomed them to relegation. The word was that Plymouth Argyle's employees hadn't been paid for months. Whilst some of the players could cope with their income stalling, the club's staff and younger players must have been feeling the pinch. It's credit to the Plymouth players that they haven't rolled over and on this display they looked like they would have been a mid-table team in any other season.

They certainly matched Posh and frustrated them in a grim first half. The visitors were out-muscling their hosts in midfield but it still came as a surprise when Carl Fletcher opened the scoring on 38 minutes as he applied the finish to Simon Walton free kick. Surely this would spur Posh into action, but David Button was the equal of whatever was on target and speculative shots from Tommy Rowe and James Wesolowski failed to even register applause from an increasingly bored London Road crowd, some of whom voiced their displeasure at half-time.

Lee Tomlin replaced Rowe during the interval and he immediately sparked some interest in the match with his close control and vision. He created chances for George Boyd and Craig Mackail-Smith and the feeling spread that an equaliser would be a formality. Ryan Bennett did the honours on 56 minutes with a sharp header from an even sharper Grant McCann cross that left Button with barely a chance to react.

Posh were finding their stride. David Ball headed wide within seconds of play resuming but Joe Lewis reacted smartly to a low drive from Yannick Bolasie. A sometimes valid criticism of

Lewis is that he can switch off after a lengthy period without seeing the ball but his concentration was resolute and more besides today.

Mark Little displayed his attacking prowess on 70 minutes with a speedy run down the right wing that left his markers trailing before cutting the ball back for Mackail-Smith to notch his 30th goal of his outstanding season.

Posh deserved their lead but Plymouth were still prepared to battle and it took an astounding save from Lewis to deny an almost certain goal from a Walton header. If you can recall Gordon Banks' save from Pele in 1970 then you are not far from what Lewis pulled off in front of a far smaller audience at London Road.

Lewis must have wanted this match to last forever. Almost everything he did was what one would expect of a highly-regarded goalkeeper and it must have been all-the-more satisfying for him after his recent mistakes and the level of criticism they inspired. Hearts leapt into mouths when he went down injured before stoppage time but he was back on his feet to offer a final moment to savour.

Deep into added time, the referee interpreted Stephane Zubar's stumble as being the result of a trip from substitute Lee Frecklington. It is widely perceived that Frecklington doesn't do much on the pitch and his phantom trip did little to knock that perception. Nevertheless, Mr Stroud felt that Frecklington had finally made his mark on Posh's season and pointed to the spot. There was nothing wrong with Luke Summerfield's well-struck spot kick but Joe Lewis concluded possibly his best match for Posh with a full-stretch save that has to go down as one of the best ever penalty stops at London Road.

Mr Stroud almost immediately blew for full time and the contrast between the reception given to Lewis today and the stoney silence after the Bournemouth match could not have been anymore stark. He had won us this match. Even one of his most enduring critics, Hugh Fat B'stard, enthusiastically endorsed this inescapable fact. We can only hope for Lewis's sake that the watching scouts hadn't bothered with the two recent matches on Sky because they'll have seen a goalkeeper at the very top of his game today.

Paul Myland

* * * * *

22/04/11

Leyton Orient 2 - 1 Peterborough United

Zakuani '67 (og) Mendez-Laing '75
Jarvis '90

Leyton Orient: *Jones, Omozusi, Forbes, Cox, Dawson, McGleish (sub Tehoue 31min), Chambers, Daniels (sub Crowe 89min), Spring, Kane (sub Jarvis 80min), Barrett. Unused subs: Whing, Butcher, Carroll, Odubajo.*
Posh: *Lewis, Little, Zakuani, Lee, Wesolowski (sub Frecklington 61min) Ball (sub Mendez-Laing 71min), Boyd, McCann, Mackail-Smith, Bennett, Tomlin. Unused subs: Langmead, Davies, Jones, Newell.*
Attendance: *5,476 (1,264 Posh fans)*

When the fixtures for the news season are published in June I always look out for when the away games to London based teams will be as this usually provides an opportunity to have a good pub crawl around our fine capital.

After becoming a father for the first time in January to another Poshie, Good Friday was earmarked as the day that I would not only watch the Posh at Leyton Orient but officially wet the baby's head. The other lads from Whittlesey were up for this one and by the time the day came around there was a healthy contingent of 10 Posh fans from Whittlesey headed to East London.

I took the 9:45 train with my old chap, brother in-law and good mate Dave, whilst the others opted for the later train. Now if there's one thing about blokes from Whittlesey is that they can certainly drink and my mate Dave is a specialist in this field. We decided to take the fast train despite this being vastly more expensive, the sole reason for this decision was that the fast train has a bar and ensured we didn't die of thirst on the way down. Four cans of Heineken were downed as we discussed the importance of today's match with the phrase "s★★t or bust" the most apt to describe it.

When we got into Kings Cross, my brother in-laws plan to take us to Liverpool St by tube was foiled by engineering work so we hopped into a taxi and headed for the Wetherspoons located just outside the station. We met up with the other bods from Whittlesey and a couple of my West Ham supporting mates. We took advantage of the cold beer on a scorching day and spent a leisurely few hours before deciding to head towards the ground.

We made for the Coach & Horses outside the ground where the long bar queue meant we had to order four pints each when we finally got served. Outside we sat in the blazing sunshine supping warm Stella out of plastic cups, but by this time we didn't care, in fact to my complete surprise I heard Dave mutter four words I thought I would never hear him say: "I can't drink anymore".

We decided to head into the ground at 2:55 and took the pleasant walk to the ground. Brisbane Road or the Matchroom Stadium as it is now called has changed drastically since my last visit when Drewe Broughton (remember him) scored a winner to give Posh a 2-1 win back in December 1998 when we were really s★★t. Posh fans were packed into the East Stand which is an old style stand and were in good numbers as we had sold the allocation of 1,300 tickets.

We took our seats to watch the game and were sparked up into life from our alcohol induced coma when Ryan Bennett smashed in a header on seven minutes only for the goal to be disallowed for a push on an Orient defender that none of us could see The first half petered out with no team taking control despite the noisy vocal encouragement from the Posh faithful.

Half way through the second-half and much against the run of play Orient took the lead when Zakuani sliced in an Orient cross. Posh looked rocked by this goal but found a way back into the game when substitute Mendez-Laing smashed in a header to make it 1-1 Now there only looked one team likely to win this game and Posh had a great chance to go in front just moments later when Boyd had a good chance blocked. As we started to leave the ground disappointed but content with a point, disaster struck when Orient scored six minutes into injury time, cue the Posh masses off home gutted that Posh had come away with nothing. As we made our way back to the tube station the general consensus among us was that automatic promotion was now out of the question for the Posh and it was the Play-Offs at best. The nature of the defeat left us all wondering whether Posh had the mental strength to secure promotion this term.

We made our way to the Aberconway Pub, refuelled, and then headed for some scran and some more beer and caught the 8pm train home. I walked through my door at 21:15 with the wife watching telly in bed and the little lad fast asleep in his bedroom. The Mrs could tell instantly from my facial expression that the Posh had lost whilst I went into see the little lad and whispered: "Posh lost mate but we'll still go up."

I'm sure he smiled back although it could have been wind, who knows...

Ben Donnelly

* * * * *

25/04/11

Peterborough United 2 - 2 Yeovil Town

Langmead '87	Wooton (pen) '23
Mackail-Smith '89	Tutte '87

Posh: *Jones, Langmead, Zakuani, Lee, Frecklington (sub Taylor 60min), Ball (sub Mackail-Smith 60min), Rowe (sub Boyd 60min), Whelpdale, Mendez-Laing, Tomlin, Newell. Unused subs: Lewis, Wesolowski, Bennett, Davies.*
Yeovil: *Henderson, Alcock, Jones, Smith, Bowditch (sub Gritton 67min), Welsh (sub Upson 83min), Ehmer, Tutte, Wotton, MacDonald, Obika. Unused subs: Stewart, Russell, Grit Gibson, Fitzsimons, Baggridge.*
Attendance: *6,489 (254 Yeovil fans)*

Good weather was forecast for the Bank Holiday Weekend which was a real bonus as Posh were at home to Yeovil on the Monday. An email then arrived from close family friends in Australia: .'Gday from Oz, coming over for a football fix can you get us some tickets for Posh v Yeovil and put us up for a few nights? Cheers Dave &Mark.

So before they arrived I emailed the club and explained about my visitors and could PUFC make their first visit to London Rd a memorable one ? Next day the club replied, asking us to be at the ground at 1pm on match day as they had arranged for us to meet fellow Australian and Posh player James Wesolowski.

The big day arrived and we were blessed with glorious sunshine. luckily for us the Bank Holiday break coincided with Charters beer festival - Posh and a beer festival and sunshine, could it get any better? On arriving at the ground we bumped into Pete Lane - the Posh historian - and introduced him to my guests and after a quick chat was told to wait a few minutes while he had a word with Sir Tommy Robson. We were then treated to a tour of the ground after a visit to the Posh changing rooms. We had our photo's taken with all the players and chatted about todays opponents and the push for promotion.

The players were great and made us feel very welcome. After the tour had finished we nipped to Charters for a few pints in the sunshine.

The teams were announced and Posh made seven changes to their starting line up, resting most of our star players and also fielding a youth team player called Joe Newell. What a let down for our visitors who had travelled half way round the world to see CMS, Boydy and Joe Lewis in action.

What a drab affair the match was, the only highlight of a boring first half was Joe Lewis's replacement Paul Jones bringing down a Yeovil player for a penalty. 1-0 to Yeovil and this did not look good, we were missing our big guns. The second half got under way with no changes to our team and the match seemed to be drifting by when a big cheer went up! The big guns were about to make their entry.

Craig Mackail-Smith, George Boyd and Paul Taylor. Who's that? I was asked, errr, errr he's a hard nut from Merseyside.

What a transformation. CMS running at defenders, Boydy with his silky skills nearly setting up Craig Mackail-Smith with his first touch - what a nightmare it must be for the defenders trying to mark them. Paul Taylor, what a box of tricks he is. And also nearly scores with his first touch, looks like we have found another gem. The pressure finally tells and Langmead scores a good goal with only a few minutes remaining when a loose ball in the area breaks kindly for him. What a relief, time surely left for us to push on and get a winner.

The London Road end now in full song are roaring us on for that final push for three much needed points if we want a decent play-off position. Yeovil have not read the script and soon after kicking off they break down the wing, cut inside past young Joe Newell and bang ... the ball is nestling in the corner of Jones' net. All goes quiet at London Rd 2-1 to Yeovil as the game moves into injury time. The fourth official holds his board above his head, four minutes of injury time. The crowd get behind the team as they have done all season and Posh respond with wave after wave of frantic pressure on the Yeovil goal. A minute to go and we get a corner, up steps Tomlin and sends a great delivery into the box, the ball is flicked on to the far post and Craig Mackail-Smith nips in to smack the ball home off his ankle/leg/knee/shin.

London Rd goes wild and soon after ref blows for full time, and what a fantastic final few minutes, it makes up for the rest of the drab match and most of the crowd went home happy with a point salvaged in stoppage time.

It was time to hit the beer and food at Charters where we met up with my wife and daughter and re-live the whole match experience over a great meal. Happy days watching the mighty Posh.

Dave Bradley

The long trek for this fixture began for me on Good Friday. I had decided to book a couple of days off work and make a bit of a holiday of the Easter Weekend, by going down to my folks and staying there for a couple of days before travelling across to Peterborough with them. However, the family home is located in the back of beyond in Mid Wales, so is not the easiest place to get to via public transport; my journey usually involves a bus to Manchester, a trudge across Manchester city centre to Piccadilly Station, then a train to Shrewsbury, which is still a good forty-five minute drive from the house.

This particular journey began with the low-cost abomination which is the Megabus. Now, I have come to expect a substandard level of hygiene on these hellish charabancs, but this bus was positively medieval. My decision to take the surprisingly vacant double-seat towards the rear backfired as, owing to a blocked toilet, the stench of day-old Scotswee wafted ominously around me like some pissy aura. I will spare the reader the gory details of what followed, but most of the journey was spent with my feet hovering a few inches above the floor. Needless to say, I was extremely relieved to reach

Manchester and get some fresh air. But, you get what you pay for, I s'pose.

Unfortunately, to add further misery, the bus was half an hour late getting in, so I subsequently had to dash across the city centre (which at least dried out the bottom of my trousers), just about catching my connecting train. Once I reached Shrewsbury, a very pleasant couple of hours was spent sat in the sun in a beer garden reading the paper, before I met my dad and we headed across into Cymru.

After a couple of days spent catching up with old friends, we set off for Peterborough on Sunday morning. The idea was to visit an old childhood haunt on the Sunday, before stopping over in Peterborough and going to the match the next day. We decided that the Sunday should be spent at Wicksteed Park, which was a regular stomping ground for my brother and I as children. Funnily enough, the place is pretty much exactly as it was when I first went twenty years ago, save for the odd lick of paint. Regrettably, it seems a lot less magical as a grown-up. In fact, I feared for my life on a few of the rides, not least the extremely fragile looking Pirate Ship. After a few hours surrounded by wasps and white trash, we made our way to Peterborough. Upon reaching our destination, we checked into The Bull (Ooooh, look at me...) before heading out into a deserted town centre for a few drinks and a very nice meal.

The day of the game started with an artery-assaulting cooked breakfast, followed by a mooch around the shops and a pint in the sun. We reached the ground soon after two, to be greeted by the news that Ferguson would be fielding a second-string team, in order to give a few of the top players a well-needed rest before the playoffs. Naturally, due to the distance travelled and the infrequency of attendance, this was a little disappointing (if completely understandable). However, on the positive side, it gave Posh fans the opportunity to see how the fringe players could perform, and the players themselves the opportunity to play themselves into first-team contention.

Unfortunately, it seems that no-one actually told the players this. Notably, Langmead was his usual clumsy self, Whelpdale was lost at right-back, Ball was nonexistent, and Nathaniel Mendez-Laing was, frankly, rubbish.

The game started scrappily, with a multitude of misplaced passes from both sides, leading to a distinct lack of football being played by either. However, a breakthrough came after half an hour. Unfortunately it was for Yeovil. A feeble header from Langmead was pounced on by the Yeovil striker who was subsequently clattered inside the area by Posh debutant, and Jugglin' Joe understudy, Paul Jones. Paul Wotton stepped up, and put Yeovil 1-0 in the lead.

The next half an hour was similarly crap, with Posh creating very little. However, the team began to spring into life on 60 minutes when London Road demigods, Craig Mackail-Smith and George Boyd, were introduced, accompanied by 'chirpy Scouser' Paul Taylor. Lee Tomlin suddenly woke up, and Posh finally looked as though they had an attacking threat, with all four looking lively. The equaliser came on 87 minutes, after Whelpdale, far more impressive in his natural right-midfield position, forced a corner which Langmead volleyed in with a finish which almost made one think that he was a striker trying to play at centre-back.

Alas, the relief was short-lived; Yeovil were back in front immediately after Tutte was given far too much space by the otherwise impressive Joe Newell and fired past the sprawling Paul Jones with a crispy shot the like of which would have the .com team clambering for its finest mixed metaphors.

I feared the worst, but I needn't have. The ever reliable Mackail-Smith appeared soon afterwards to slot in another equaliser following a comedic goalmouth scramble thus securing a meaningless point in a typically end-of-season affair.

If this game is going to remembered at all, it will be for the performance of hitherto unknown 17 year old debutant, Joe Newell, who, defensive lapse aside, looked assured, comfortable on the ball and technically astute. Oh, and the Moy's was opened up for home fans, for the very last time before the bulldozers move in (ha-ha).

With many hackneyed clichés in mind for my report, we ventured back to Wales, where I stopped overnight, before continuing back up to Glasgow the next day.

The toilet on the Megabus was still broken.

Pat McDevitt, Glasgow

* * * * *

30/04/11

Rochdale 2 - 2 Peterborough United

Akpa-Apro '1 Mendez-Laing '45
Dawson '87 Tomlin '46

Rochdale: *Fon Williams, Wiseman, Widdowson, Holness, Josh Thompson, Barry-Murphy, Kennedy (sub Jones 48min), Done, Joe Thompson (sub O'Grady 50min), Akpa-Akpro, Adams (sub Dawson 74min). Unused subs: Edwards, Flynn, Williams, Atkinson.*
Posh: *Lewis, Zakuani, Lee, Bennett, Whelpdale, Boyd, Tomlin (sub Ball 86min), McCann, Mendez-Laing (sub Davies 83min), Wesolowski, Mackail-Smith. Unused subs: Jones, Taylor, Frecklington, Newell, Langmead.*
Attendance: *3,147*

All season long we had been looking forward to Posh's last away game and wondering if this would be another promotion clincher just like Hereford and Colchester. We had considered borrowing a minibus to transport all of our mates who would no doubt come crawling out of the woodwork for this massive game. We even wondered if Rochdale's 3,500-seater away stand would be big enough for the hordes of Poshies who would most likely cause traffic chaos on the M62. In reality, automatic promotion had long gone by the time this fixture came around and only my mates Steve and Woodston Bob and I joined the 400 or so other Posh fans at Spotland.

The day started as most of our Posh away days do: with a greasy fry-up at Ferrari's café on Mayors Walk. Not the finest of restaurants it has to be said, but the fact that Posh have a strange knack of winning when we go there means it has become an essential part of our away game experience.

We hit the road and by noon we had already arrived in 'Dale. An early start was essential because as many Posh fans know, the pubs in Rochdale are worth devoting a bit of time to. However, when we discovered that the Cemetery had a beer festival on, I really began to regret my decision to drive!

A few 'Dale fans already seemed to be well oiled by the time we got there – in fact, judging by the state of them, they looked like they'd been there all night for a lock-in and were already in full voice. As another Posh fan commented, it looked like the cast of Shameless on a night out. After a few games of pool we sat outside in the sun, sampled some of the local brews and looked forward to a good match in a proper, old fashioned football ground.

A while later, as we took our seats in Spotland and settled down to watch Posh kick off in the sunshine, we were completely relaxed and enjoying the prospect of seeing a game where we didn't have to fret about the result for a change. After all, we knew we were in the play offs whatever happened, so this didn't matter. Did it?

11 seconds later the ball was in the back of Posh's net and as we looked on in disbelief we decided that maybe this game did matter a little bit after all. In fact, with the play-offs looming, if Big Joe was going to start suicidally passing the ball straight to opposition strikers inside our own penalty area, it mattered a lot!

The embarrassing comedy goal seemed to cause Posh to spend the first 20 minutes of the game looking punch drunk and just as stunned as the fans as Rochdale began to enjoy some good attacking play. With both of Posh's first choice full backs missing it looked a little too easy for them to get at Posh down the flanks. However, Posh improved as the half went on as Mendez-Laing, enjoying a rare start, beat his man a couple of times. Eventually, it was NML himself who got the equaliser just before half time, heading home a McCann corner. The only other highlight of the first-half was seeing the same group of Rochdale fans we had seen in the pub earlier being ejected for fighting amongst themselves.

The second-half saw a bit of an improvement and eventually Posh took the lead, with Boydie doing what he does best, tearing down the wing, taunting his defender with a few tricks and pulling the ball back for Tomlin to fire home from the edge of the box.

However, Posh being Posh, that was not that and some more questionable defending and goalkeeping saw Rochdale bundle home a late equaliser which they probably deserved. However, as we had done our bit to ensure a Posh victory by having breakfast at Ferrari's, we still understandably felt a little bit robbed.

As we continued our day of healthy eating by tucking into a KFC at Hartshead Moor services, we decided that if Posh were to succeed in the play-offs, they would have to raise their game and play a lot better than this - and thank goodness they did. We also decided that if we were to go up to a league full of generic all-seater grounds situated in out of town industrial estates, then Rochdale would be the away day we would miss more than any other.

Richard Clay

* * * * *

May 2011

07/05/11

Peterboro' United 5 - 0 Dagenham & Redbridge

Mendez-Laing '11
McCann '65
Boyd '82
Mackail-Smith '84
Ball '90

Posh: *Lewis, Little, Zakuani, Lee (sub Newell 28min), Wesolowski (sub Ball 68min), Boyd, McCann, Rowe, Mackail-Smith, Bennett, Mendez-Laing (sub Whelpdale 80min). Unused subs: Jones, Langmead, Davies, Taylor.*
Dagenham: *Roberts, Antwi, Arber, Akinde (sub Savage 68min), Nurse, Ifil, Currie, Taiwo, Vincelot, Ilesanmi (sub Green 68min), Gain (sub Lee 78min). Unused subs: Lewington, Doe, Scannell, Walsh.*
Attendance: *7,519 (1,005 Daggers fans)*

What could have been a dead rubber game, played on cruise control to ensure that everyone was fit and avoided suspension for the upcoming play-off games now took on several factors directly impacting on the look of the table. The Daggers needed at least a draw to stand any chance of avoiding the drop straight back into League Two. This wasn't the first time that I had been to a game where the threat of relegation added to the tension and made it one of the results that would have fans across the country nervously keeping tabs on their radios/phones for the latest news.

There was another question to be settled of course, who would we end up facing in the play-offs? With Huddersfield having gone on an epic unbeaten run since losing to Arsenal in the FA Cup in January, leaving them secure in third, it was pretty much a straight fight between Bournemouth and the MK D.....no, sorry, can't do it, the Imposters Whilst confident that we could maintain our proud record of having never lost a play off game, there were pro's and cons on both sides. Bournemouth would have been easier for me to get to get to for the away leg as Milton Keynes is a transport nightmare no matter which way you look at it.

What made this game all the more special was that it was the first game that I was going to be able to attend this season having moved to Bristol the previous summer, making the 500 mile round journey just as hard on my wallet as my butt following an average six hours sitting on coaches. There were of course newly local away days to be had at Bristol Rovers and Yeovil, but a combination of illness (Rovers) and postponements due to the weather (Yeovil) meant that I had had to settle for the life of an armchair fan. There was also the ex-Poshie factor to consider...not only did they have Peter Gain and Mark Arber playing for them, but also, there was John Still, who if management skills were based on whether you were a nice bloke or not would be managing Barcelona but unfortunately (for us *and* him) he had to follow in the footsteps of the calamitous Lil Fuccillo.

It was just as well that I set out back to Peterborough on Friday to allow myself some time to acclimatise to the flatness of the Fens as once again my lack of punctuality cost me dear. Thinking that I had five minutes to spare, I rocked up to the bus station in Bristol just in time to see my coach heading to Birmingham rolling out of the forecourt before double checking my ticket and realising that I had had the times for the London coaches in my head leaving me stranded and needing a miracle to make the connecting train at the other end. Aplogetic texts were sent to mates waiting in the pub and I wandered off to the internet cafe to further line the retirement fund of National Express shareholders and book *another* couple of coaches to get me back.

Arriving six hours later than planned I embarked upon my traditional homecoming routine of heading straight to the

Wortley for possibly one of the last places where you can get change from £2 for a pint. Unfortunately, I found that most of my mates had already gone home or were already smashed.

Usually following a session such as was had the night before, there's little chance of seeing much meaningful movement before midday, but this was different, there was a game to get to and so it was that I rose with the giddy anticipation of a kid on Christmas Day, I was off to the Posh. Not being even vaguely interested in football, my mate Clare did at least pay lip service to my excitement by asking a few questions about the game and listened in to yet another passionate rant about the Imposters and why they were hated so much...bless her. Having left later than planned, there wasn't time to make it over to Ebenezeers for a pre-match pint and get round to sorting my PISA membership, so having dropped Clare off at Charters with friends taking in the music going on, started my wander towards the ground.

Ever since going to my first game back in 1986 with my Dad against Cambridge I have always loved the buzz that you get from seeing the ground as you cross the bridge and approach the turnstiles. With only five minutes to go before the KO, the queues were mercifully short at the London Road end and soon I was reminded of the horror that are the gents toilets.

Having headed for *my* spot since the days when I could afford to go regularly in the 89/90 season (just to the right of the goal, about half way back), I soaked up the atmosphere as the players names were announced and was suitably impressed that the family stand was close to capacity and it seemed that the Daggers had bought a fair few fans along for the ride too.

As ever, I couldn't help but check out what Peter Burrow was up to these days having been one of the previous incarnations back in the day when our season was being 'saved' from going off the rails, after the sacking of Mark Wright. Damn, I wish I was still in the suit as there's nothing to compare to the buzz of running out onto the pitch with the players!

Early doors, the action ebbed and flowed a bit as both teams tried to find a rythym to their passing, but following a beautiful ball down the channel for Mendez-Laing to chase onto, he skinned Arber for pace and placed the ball past the keeper into the net to make 1-0. This should have been the cue to relax, but this is the Posh with a defence that had conceded more goals than just about anyone else in the country, never mind the division. Everytime they managed to break out and get near the box, there was a collective sense of panic that seemed to engulf the crowd never mind the defence .

At half-time, the general opinion was that CMS might be feeling the pressure of helping to relegate a previous club where he had a special affinity but generally I was quite happy with where we were at from experience of Fergie's previous reign, I was holding out hope for a storming second half and another couple of goals, the question being...at which end?

The general consensus is that you have to be a nutter and thicker skinned than a rhino to be a keeper, especially since for half of your working life, you know that your going to have to take at least 45 minutes of abuse from the home fans, especially if as was the case with Tony Roberts, you aren't quite as athletic as your outfield players and carry a bit of weight. Initially taking the standard issue abuse about being a 'fat bast★★d' well and funnily enough, refusing the offer to give us a dance or tell the crowd the score he then managed to keep the scoreline down as the second half got under way. CMS continued his Duracell bunny audition while managing not to score. As things stood, the Daggers were still going down and having missed the half-time scores, I was no wiser to who or where we would be heading for the play-offs.

Eventually after the second goal went in, the floodgates opened and once again, London Road was the banker for the man who liked to tick the box saying +2.5 goals per game on the bookies slip as McCann and Boyd added goals two and three. This pretty much finished the game as a contest, condemning the Daggers to relegation and when Roberts went down injured, there was genuine feeling behind the call out that 'Roberts is a legend!' because, despite near constant barracking, the goalie had taken it all on the chin and had indeed gotten his 'tits out for the lads'.

Goal number four was a personal highlight due to the combination of our new lad Newell breaking down the left to put in the sweetest of crosses for CMS to put his head onto the ball and score. To really rub the salt into the wounds, David Ball came off of the bench and finished the job off.

As the players did a lap of honour it was all about one man, and I don't mind admitting that despite a brief flirtation with George Boyd, Craig Mackail-Smith had, over the previous couple of years, inspired in me the kind of man-love normally saved for extended stays at 'Her Majestys Pleasure'. He and I both left the ground with the sound of 'WE DON'T WANT YOU TO GO, OH CRAIG MACKAIL-SMITH, WE DON'T WANT YOU TO GO' ringing in our ears.

Phil Jeffery

* * * * *

15/05/11

MK Dons 3 - 2 Peterborough United

Powell '47	Mackail-Smith '8
Baldock '50	McCann (pen) '81
Balanta '56	

MK Dons: *Martin, Lewington, Doumbe, Mackenzie, Gleeson, Baldock, Clayton, Balanta (sub Ibehre 79min), Chadwick, Powell (sub Marsh-Brown 77min). Unused subs: Guy, Searle, Woodards, G. Baldock, Chicksen.*

Posh: *Lewis (sub Jones 46min), Little, Lee, Zakuani (sub Langmead 31min), Bennett, McCann, Rowe, Tomlin, Boyd, Mackail-Smith, Mendez-Laing (sub Ball 60min). Unused subs: Whelpdale, Davies, Newell, Wesolowski.*
Attendance: *12,662 (4,319 Posh fans)*

Stadium MK, 3-1 down and looking like we could be mullered, Joe inherits a set of crutches, Gabby has to give up doing hand stands and Charlie impersonates Paul Scholes .... it looks bad.

Suddenly ….. Litt's decides to impersonate a cross between Usain Bolt and Stanley Matthews and goes off on a mazy lung bursting dribble down the right wing. He leaves two imposters in his wake and cuts infield and heads towards the penalty area.

The rest is history ... two yards outside the box he is brought down by an aggressive dislodged tuft of grass that went in with blades showing and quite rightly Gleeson is sent off and Grant slams the penalty home ... 3-2, final whistle and it felt like a win.

That was the moment for me when I fancied we would go all the way and be confident about it.

Bob Symms

As soon as Grant McCann scored the penalty to pull it back to 3-2, you could sense the MK Dons players realising that they'd have to avoid conceding at London Road, something which only Brighton had done all season. Their fans could feel it too. That goal was as good as an equaliser and I am not alone in leaving Milton Keynes simply knowing that Posh would get the two goals necessary to secure the trip to Old Trafford. It certainly made being stuck in the tailbacks on the road to Bedford seem worthwhile.

Paul Myland

* * * * *

19/05/11

Peterborough United 2-0 MK Dons

McCann '11
Mackail-Smith '54

***Posh:** Jones, Little, Zakuani, Wesolowski, Boyd, McCann (sub Whelpdale 70min), Mackail-Smith, Rowe, Bennett, Tomlin, Basey. Unused subs: Richardson, Langmead, Ball, Mendez-Laing, Davies, Newell.*
***MK Dons:** Martin, Lewington, Doumbe, Mackenzie, O'Hanlon (sub Guy 86min), Gleeson, Baldock, Balanta, Clayton, Chadwick (sub Ibehre 65min), Powell (sub Marsh-Brown 65min). Unused subs: Searle, Woodards, G. Baldock, Chicksen.*
***Attendance:** 11,920 (2,005 Dons fans)*

The day starts early for me – I'm awake at 04.30am. For crying out loud I'm far too old for this. My head is buzzing about tonight and all that it means. I've arranged to be 'working from home for today, so I have the school run first up and I'm greeted by Mum's and Dad's all keen to know if we're going tonight - even in leafy St Albans tonight's game has significance. As we are the token Posh fans in the playground we become the centre of attention. "Do you think you'll win?", "are you taking Sam and George?" my stock responses are "yes, provided the real Posh turn up tonight - we can't play as badly again as last Sunday" and "their mother said – Posh on a school night? No way - we said way…"

I get back from dropping off and go straight onto the on-line fans forums, eager to sniff out any snippet of information regarding tonight. Truth is both managers are tighter as a drum on tonight's team selections or anything else of significance. Whilst Darren is working his psychological genius on the players psyche a feelgood thread to raise the spirits of the fans on londonroad.net and various contributions are flying in for music, inspirational speeches and flashbacks to past days of Posh glory. There are also many references the game against Gillingham in 1974 with Engelbert's 'The Last Waltz' featuring highly. The effect is immense and suddenly the usual dour online mood is transformed. Everyone is upbeat and united behind the team. My contribution to work through the course of the day is the square root of not very much.

I pick Sam and George up at 3pm from school and their excitement is apparent - they get changed in the car as we head North up the A1, we have my iTunes Posh playlist for background music and I'm talking to my boys about tonight. How that every 10 years or so these games come along so you have to make the most of them when they do. I talk about previous play-offs and how that if we play like we can, tonight will live long in their memory.

Just as Gillingham, 1974 does with me. I explained how at that game I was on my Dad's shoulders, on the pitch, celebrating as Tommy Robson, Chris Turner, Bert Murray, John Cozens, Jim Hall, Fred Hill and Noel Cantwell and the other heroes from that night were all partying in the Director's box. Those of us on the pitch were going totally chicken oriental too, in a mid '70s style - complete with flairs, tank tops and bad haircuts.

We arrive and grab a pizza, before getting into the ground early. The stadium, with the exception of the Moy's End, is packed and the tension is immense. In a master-stroke of crowd management, previous Posh play-off heroes are paraded out to an adoring London Road. I explain to Sam and George who these players are and what they achieved, inevitably the crowd erupts into a chorus of "you've got no history, you've got no history ..." and so the scene is then set for an evening bristling with antipathy towards MK Dons. Game on. I swear you could see sparks generated by the atmosphere.

The game kicks off and the noise generated is as loud as I can remember with all three Posh sides of the ground in full voice. I pass around our dods – mint humbugs, then Fadge behind me hands out eclairs. Moments Sam later is spitting toffee, chocolate, blood, saliva ... and a tooth. "Don't worry son, you'll be fine …" I say in hope. "You'll blame me for that …" mutters Fadge – he was oh so right.

The game is intense and the early exchanges are closely fought. Pay attention boys, we could score here … YES!!!!! Grant McCann curls in his free kick over the wall, 1-0 to Posh. Everyone bar the Moy's End goes wild, the tension is eased. This could be our night.

The second half continues in similar vein to the first and it's Posh that continue to hold the game by the scruff of the neck. That grip is tightened when Boyd's shot is blocked and then pounced upon by, who else, Craig Mackail-Smith. The patron Saint of lost causes has added clinical poacher to his armoury of skills and takes his 34th goal of the season. 2-0 Posh, we are going through with this scoreline.

Not content to defend what we have, Posh use attack as the best form of defence and continue to press. Our back five are immense tonight. Tomlin has what would have been a well taken third goal disallowed when advantage was not played. This party was not going to be spoilt though and the incident merely served to unite the crowd further, and as the volume lifted once more Posh pressed again.

The whole atmosphere was relentless and as each minute passed we got louder and more behind the team. Clearly this was getting to MK and was best displayed when Gleeson threw a hissy-fit at Marsh-Brown. Much to the delight of the home fans. The clock counted down and euphoric scenes erupted as realisation dawned – Posh had played as we all knew they could. We had performed in front of a massive audience and the cameras. A trip to Old Trafford was secured.

The crowd spilled onto the pitch and half-hearted attempts were made to prevent the spontaneous invasion, my sons were standing on their seats either side of me. We were delirious. A tear of joy rolled down my cheek whilst my boys witnessed Posh history, my youngest George asked: "are you alright Dad?" all at that point was just perfect. But it got so much better.

"Dad, dad can we go on the pitch too?" I didn't have to think twice and we made our way downstairs. The party atmosphere was addictive and echos of that night in '74 were all around. We were on the pitch and I stood with Sam perched on one shoulder and George on the other (for as long as I could manage), cheering the players wildly celebrating in the directors box.

The Last Waltz rang out once again around London Road, as it had in '74. This was a circle of life moment and will always stay with Sam, George and myself. It was priceless. I'm sure you were watching from up there Dad, and I'm certain you were feeling as proud as I was.

Chris Sharpe

I hate the imposters. I hate their plastic no character stadium. Their supporters don't know how to behave so add nothing to the atmosphere either home or away.

We could have been thrashed at their place but they took their foot off the pedal so obviously that scouse dwarf knows nothing either and their chairman and board pissed off Darragh by cavorting around the boardroom after the game as though they were already in the Championship.

So yes I loathe them. I couldn't wait for the second leg at a proper football stadium in front of proper supporters. I was not let down at any stage from the surprisingly early time I got in the London Road End up to kick off and all game.

I would honestly say that for an old fart like me the atmosphere came very close to that great night in 74 when we sealed the Division 4 title in front of over 18,000. We all know what happened during the game and how as one the fans and players frightened the shit out of the Imposters. Their supporters were silent but we all knew they would be but to see previously gobby players in their ranks reduced to bit part actors in the drama gave me a warm glow.

I am proud to be Posh at any time but that night made me as proud as ever I have been. The Stellas were flowing later on that night in Ebeneezer's and the toast was for once aimed at the Posh fans aswell as that heroic team.

God I love my football club.

Adi Mowles

I don't ever remember a Posh match where I had felt so nervous and tense before kick-off. Even the walk from the pub to LR, usually filled with lots of chat about the days game and beyond, was pretty silent. All caught up with our own thoughts wondering what if, and mainly "we can't lose to them!"

The match is a blur of goals and misses without too many worries in the end, and on that final whistle it was man hugs all round and walking out onto the pitch. That night, I still refused to even think about Old Trafford, it was enough to bask in the glow of what the whole club - players, fans, Darragh - had achieved. My favourite ever night at London Road.

Jamie Jones

After singing myself hoarse, I couldn't resist running onto the pitch afterwards despite being in the upper tier of the Family Stand. I had almost fractured a bone in my left foot whilst out running nine days before but the pain wasn't going to stop me racing down the Family Stand stairs. But bugger me, it didn't half hurt when I reached the pitch. Tonight, the pain simply didn't matter.

Paul Myland

At 71 years of age it it gets pretty hard to stay awake until midnight and then for an hour and a half to follow the game on the BBC "live" scores. It is better when the chat room is open but even then I quickly start to nod off. I have to make do with getting up anytime after 5 am on Sunday morning and reading as many reports as possible of the game played last night. My mood for the rest of the day is determined by the result of the game.

But for the play offs this year it was all different. For the first time ever I was able to watch Posh live on the television. Fox Sports showed the games live here in Brisbane!! It's almost unbelievable. I told everybody who would listen and I have to say that not many were overly interested. But I was.

And what a great time I had watching - especially the game against MK Dons at London Road and of course the final at Old Trafford. I was a bundle of nerves watching them both. The MK Dons game started at about 4:45am here which meant that all I had to do was get up early.

At 5 am the Posh scored and the aggregate scores were equal. One of my neighbours told me later that he was awakened by my shouting. At about 5:30am I posted to the LondonRoad.net message board "I'm just not used to this tension. Every time MK get the ball I am a nervous wreck. 1-0 at half time. We need another goal to settle my nerves a bit."

At about 6 am the second goal came and I was so delirious I made myself another cup of coffee. At 6:52 am I posted "Some of the people lucky enough to have been there will be home soon. It will be good to hear from them." and I waited at the computer for the reports to come in. And come in they did. All of them were full of praise for the Posh and it made great reading for me.

Tony Pell, Brisbane, Australia

19/05/11

Having seen MK off in the return on the Thursday night - and what a night of passion and pride it was with London Road rocking - the lead- up to the final was a mixture of calm and chaos (organised that is). The Manager and the players went about training, oozing buckets of confidence and really enjoying the moment, automatic promotion is good for the heart-rate but there's something special about Play-Off Finals at this club.

Behind the scenes it's manic, tickets, new shirts, new sponsor, coaches to Manchester, suits, hotels, shop, programmes, Old Trafford info, etc, etc, but the whole place is alive with anticipation ... and so are the fans.

27/05/11

Early morning and the lads are packed off to Carrington, it's a stunning facility and the perfect place to go through final planning and shape, mind you certain individuals (who will not be named) forget all sorts of items that could be useful ... suits tickets and ...even boots!

28/05/11

Its early evening and nearly 40 of us are in a private room at the hotel with a giant

screen, it's time to watch the first half of a unique family double that will take in two Cup Finals, first its Man U versus Barcelona.

Whilst the game is a master-class in technique and control, the near 70% / 30% possession stats and 3-1 score-line tell their own story ... as David Villa bends his shot superbly into the top corner for the third goal one of our party uttered something about spherical objects and left for bed.

His day would come tomorrow.

Bob Symms

* * * * *

29/05/11

Huddersfield Town 0 - 3 Peterborough United

Rowe '78
Mackail-Smith '80
McCann '85

Huddersfield: *Bennett, Hunt, Kay, Clarke, Naysmith, Kilbane, Peltier, Arfield (sub Lee 82min), Ward (sub Cadarmateri 79min), Roberts, Afobe (sub Rhodes 82min). Unused subs: Colgan, McCombe, Gudjonsson, Novak.*
Posh: *Jones, Little, Basey (sub Lee 63min), Zakuani, Bennett, Wesolowski, McCann, Boyd, Tomlin (sub Ball 85min), Rowe (sub Whelpdale 85min), Mackail-Smith. Unused ubs: Richardson, Langmead, Mendez-Laing, Newell.*
Attendance: 48,410 (15,111 Posh fans)

Saturday morning 7am and the missus and I arrive at Gatwick to be met by Sanj, my driver, to set off on the 300 mile journey to Manchester. To be honest I'm still not myself and haven't been since we played MK in the second leg. Call it stress, pressure, expectation or fear of failure but the whole play off situation has taken over my life. If another person says: 'Its the best way to be promoted' or 'Don't worry about it as its been magnificent just to get there' etc I will f**king explode in a rage not seen since the Incredible Hulk first went Green.

Even on the three hour drive I am thinking of OT and the possible outcomes good or bad. There is so much on the line and winning would be a vindication of changing managers at a critical moment and the pay off for a big gamble our club took this season.

Around 10am we pull up to hotel and I pop out and walk into the lobby only to be met with around 30 players in new Nike training kit waiting to go training like they are preparing for a f**king friendly the following day. The Gaffer and Rooster come over and we chew the fat for 10 minutes whilst the lads board the bus to Carrington training ground. I cannot believe how chilled everyone is and almost like there is an air of dare I say ‘Belief’ in all of them that we will win at OT. I wish this atmosphere could be bottled as I’d drink the f**ker for the rest of the day. Arrangements are made to all meet in private room at 7pm to watch United in their big game. I head off to my room where the Missus can distract me for next eight or nine hours. Meet up with the squad and management for the United game and again enjoyable and low key and talk to lots of lads who are still very chilled 15 hours before the ‘Biggest game of their Lives’.

Sunday morning 11.30am and I am dressed and ready for action. Stick my Mom’s earrings into my pocket for luck -took them to MK game so she was with me in spirit - and have a smoke outside the hotel lobby. Best sight of the day was seeing all the players’ wives, families and kids come and spend time with them a few hours before kick off. And now I am worrying about them to and how this match will affect them personally.

More stress. Bob then tells me as a heads-up that Huddersfield have been at OT since 7am and stuck banners around the ground, T-shirts on every chair and little signs with word ‘Believe’ on them as well. Wonderful, I say to myself, they already have 40,000 people there against our 15 or 16,000 and now are really going all out to gee up their fans. Barry sees I am little perturbed about it and reminds me its 11 vs 11 and that means we should win. Fair point. Anyhow I wish the lads well, have a quiet word with the Gaffer thanking him for the journey so far.

1pm arrive at ground and we’re met by fans waiting for the bus to arrive who give us a warm welcome. Go up to the lovely hospitality area and step out into stand to see the blue and white plastered everywhere. Get told I can’t go and drain the stallion as the Football League chairman is to make his speech. He gets my name wrong when reading speech out and one of main sponsors for nPower has a few words including the fact he is a Huddersfield fan. I cant take all the waiting around so I go for smoke outside only to be met by loads of Posh fans who want pictures and offer incredible support. Then I get abused by some Huddersfield fans on the way back in. Receive my usual text from my Pops back in the States which reads ' 3-1 to the posh, enjoy' to which I text back ' They ain't going to f**king score'. Then I meet some scruffy fella' from the Standing on the Glebe podcast and ask him how the f**k did he sneak in here.

3pm. We take our seats with the missus holding my hand tight and now the tension is even getting to her. I see all the fans and so badly want the win for them as they are incredible. I end up with two Football League fellas sitting next to me boxing me in and think 'typical'. I can't even curse or scream obscenities or these two will hit us with fines. First-half we should be two up by it doesn't happen. Second-half starts with 20 of the longest minutes of my life as we are on the back foot and they have all the momentum but luckily are still not creating any chances. We break away and get a free kick which the skipper delivers with gusto which just needs anybody to touch. Everyone is jumping up celebrating and I'm stuck to my seat trying to read how much time is left on the clock. I think it's 12 or 11 minutes and by time I have figured it out Boydy is on the march and pulls it back for Smudger to knock in for 2-0.

Do I celebrate now or still shitting myself as we have had habit of nicking defeat from jaws of victory this season. Only when Grant put us 3-0 up do I celebrate like crazy and the gravity of this day and achievement has sunk in. I am actually crying internally sat there staring into space when Baz drags me off my seat down towards the dug out.

4.55 – 5.55: one of best hours of my life celebrating on the pitch with all the lads and our fans and taking in the moment which you never want to stop. We go into the dressing rooms and the celebrations continue, do some press and have some words amongst us about what this means. I head back towards Directors lounge and see Lee Tomlin holding my trophy and wrestle it from him and take it upstairs into the lounge. All our guests up there go gaga for it and have pictures taken and on it goes.

I pop back outside to look at pitch one last time and see Dean the Huddersfield Owner and his son sitting in stand on their own. I go over and sit with them and the feeling of jubilation and success is gone and replaced with one of pure empathy for a great man and his son who above all are Huddersfield fans. He is incredibly graceful and we chat about next year and I tell him I'll be rooting for him and Lee to win the League. Banners, t shirts and believe signs aside, they are two great fellas who deserve success, and quickly. Outside the stadium with the Trophy under my arm I run into Adi Durham who wants his photo taken with his son and is over the moon.

6pm: Back to hotel room for private moment with the Missus and the trophy. A great half-hour to be fair.

6.30pm–3am: F★★king madness as we all let our hair down in hotel after I stick £7,000 behind the bar for everyone to drink what they want. I sit with the Gaffer and Barry and we just take in the moment. Throughout the night I spend time with all the lads and their families and really get to know some of them. F★★king heroes every last one of them. Then I'm off to bed with the trophy and missus for an hours sleep before dropping her off at the airport back in London. I could say more about those great eight hours but best left there in Manchester!

Job f★★king done, stress is lifted and work now starts on making our team a well run championship football club and keeping our fans happy.

Three promotions in four years it is then.

Darragh MacAnthony

And so to Old Trafford. The self-styled Theatre of Dreams. It's another new ground for me to tick off, but I wish we were at Wembley. For a start, in London we might not be outnumbered 2:1 by Huddersfield fans.

The semi-final (the second leg) was memorable night - an

electric atmosphere at London Road and a performance to match from the players. If this was to be the final high-point of the year, that would be OK, it's hard to see how we could get much higher.

So I went into the Huddersfield game feeling calm, serene even, the game didn't really matter. We had defeated the forces of darkness in the semi-final and there was a serious argument that the club would be better served by another year in League 1 - not one I entirely agreed with, but there was enough to suggest that defeat wouldn't mean the end of the world.

Huddersfield, on the other hand, felt that promotion was an inevitability. They were on the most ridiculous unbeaten run (including scraping a draw against us at their place) that convinced their fans they couldn't lose. Coupled with 30,000 or so fans to roar them home, it probably wasn't even worth us turning up.

But I went anyway, because as the clichés say it really was XI v XI – and if our XI played to their full potential then they were the match of any team in the league and certainly much better than Huddersfield.

I imagine most of this book's accounts of the big day will involve a drinking session that started around Thursday lunchtime, peaked at 2.45pm on Sunday (and then began again at about 6pm). Not for me though. My mate Simon usually accompanies me to such games – he says he not a Posh fan, but he is really and we leave that as an unspoken truth. He has followed us all over the country and become indoctrinated - as if by osmosis. Anyway, the silly arse booked a holiday and stood me up. I do know other Posh fans, but there are none I would necessarily want to (or know well enough to) spend the day with, and more to the point, I am certain that the feeling would be more than mutual.

Anyway, my eldest daughter Maisie (see Boyd, Sweat and Beers – Hartlepool at home. She's not been since) expressed an interest. Wife and youngest daughter were assigned a shopping trip and this became even better when the Lowry Outlet Mall was discovered.

By Sunday morning the serenity had disappeared and I was in an advanced state of excitement – it was 1992 all over again. We set off early for the girls' swimming lessons – I needed some normality to keep me calm – and passed the only other Posh fans we know in Sleaford fortifying themselves with a Maccies breakfast. My wife (a Lincoln City fan) even expressed regret that she wasn't going – the excitement was infectious.

We got to the ground at about 1.20pm and thought we'd have a little look around and then the heavens opened. With it showing no sign of abating we headed into the ground and wondered what to do for the next hour and a half. Standing in the concourse shivering was Maisie's choice of activity and for a little while I was concerned that she didn't want to be there.

My initial reaction, as we climbed into the ground for the first time, was how small Old Trafford looked. Other stadia of similar capacity that I have been to – Wembley, the Olympic Stadium in Rome – were enormous, cavernous edifices, but Old Trafford looked like a 'normal' ground; maybe one that had been on steroids, but normal nonetheless. The next thing that we saw were the acres of blue and white – at that time t-shirts on the back of seats, rather than the backs of people – and it made for a great effect. The sheer number of Huddersfield fans really hit home for a moment. Early on though, before two o'clock, there were more Poshies in the ground than Hudds fans and it was hard to tell when they arrived – they just slipped on the t-shirts and blended into the background.

By half-past two the ground was filling rapidly and starting to rock. The announces came on: the Huddersfield bloke spoke about winning the Championship in the 1920's and then played Elvis; the Posh fella messed up his timings and ended up trying to announce the best of the team over the Last Waltz. An inauspicious start and not up to the Premier League standards expected at Old Trafford.

As the players came out, the differences in the crowds didn't seem to matter. Whilst we might not be talking outnumbering of 'Zulu' proportions, the Posh fans seemed to sense that a greater effort was needed – everybody making the noise of two, drowning out the Huddersfield fans, at least from our end.

As ever with these things, the game went by in a blur. Within a couple of minutes CMS should have put us one up and what seemed like a couple of minutes later he should have scored again – that second chance coming just before half-time. We had had all of the first half and comfortably outplayed the now not so cocky Terriers.

I was concerned that we had nothing to show for the dominance – Huddersfield surely couldn't continue to be this impotent? They weren't. They stepped up the pace in the second half and had plenty of the play but to my mind never really threatened.

Maisie had started to enjoy herself, but I was worried about the effect another half hour might have on her mood. Turns out I didn't need to worry. I don't think there's any need for me to describe the goals, if you've bought this book the chances are you a) were there and/or b) have watched them over and over and over.

When the first went in there was an explosion of joy (Maisie's first instinct was to cover her ears), followed by a collective head-turn to the scoreboard to see how long was left. Seconds later, the second goal caused the biggest outpouring of ecstasy that I think I have ever seen. There were body parts everywhere – a bouncing, screaming mass of humanity.

I picked Maisie up and gave her the kind of squeeze that would normally alert Child Services and she returned with interest. Now this was it, she had let herself go and was really hooked.

Huddersfield were crushed. Finished. We scored again, but this time the celebrations were triumphal rather than ecstatic. I picked up the man in the seat in front of me – above my head, the coursing adrenaline giving me superhero strength. He didn't mind; I don't think he really wanted putting down.

The Huddersfield fans started fighting amongst themselves and the equally disappointed, but less violent, started to throw their t-shirts onto the pitch. They had stopped believing.

At the final whistle I allowed myself a brief celebration before we turned and left. I made a quick call to arrange a suitable meeting point and then we shut up. There were two Posh fans amongst 30,000 miserable looking Huddersfield fans, many of whom looked like they wanted to hit something. Hard.

Discretion got the better of valour. After all, I didn't really have time to deal with them all.

Stuart Lee

Well the plan worked perfectly, we organised the Free Kicks Foundation fundraiser - walking from Barnet to Wembley via all other London grounds - to finish the weekend at the Play Off Final on the off-chance that Posh would be there waiting for us. But there was a snag; Posh did their bit but UEFA had decided there would be another less important match at the home of football that weekend and moved the game north to Old Trafford. A quick rethink and we pulled the event a day forward, well, we didn't want to miss the one of the greatest day in our club's history did we?

So after 75 miles walking round London - 54 for some of us with bad toes who struggled on the last day - there was a calmness about the drive up to Manchester and the pre-match atmosphere around the ground, nothing like the nerves before both semi-finals against MK. How many times does a member of the Ferguson family lose at Old Trafford eh? What could go wrong?

We met up with some of our fellow walkers for a quick photo-opp before finding our seats behind the goal. Maybe it was the pain in the feet, but there was still that calmness for me. Then, what an amazing seven minutes in the second-half, no time to get nervous after the first goal, the second came so quickly, then the third. I feel privileged to have been at Old Trafford for that Beckham free kick against Greece, now Grant McCann has done it too. I screamed, I cried, I hugged everybody, that was the moment we knew we were up.

We hung about for a bit afterwards around the player's exit, managed to get a chat with Gaby, Charlie and a couple of the other heroes of the day, even bumping into a couple of ex players in Aaron Mclean and Shaun Batt. Highlight I think was seeing the HUDDERSFIELD TOWN LEAGUE 1 PLAY OFF WINNERS board being removed from the stadium. About as much use as those Believe t-shirts.

Steve Thorpe

The day stared of with me going swimming. When swimming finished we got in the car for the long journey. We had a scarf hanging out the window, we tried to count how many cars we saw with scarf's but we soon lost track. My dad told told me that Eddie Stobarts brought good luck, and Norbets bought bad luck. We saw 4 Eddies and 1 Norbet. So we hoped for good luck. When we finally got there my Mum dropped us of and we walked to Old Trafford. When we got there it was raining but my Dad said the sun came out for every play-off. When got to our seats the sun started to come out and by the time the game started it was sunny. I stood up on my chair every time something happened, I fell of my chair a few times it was all very exciting and when it got to the second half-it got even more exciting. I thought I would have to stay another half-hour till about the last 20 mins and then we scored the whole place went crazy about 5 mins later we scored again and it was even more crazy. I thought the score would be 2-0 till we scored again. The score ended up being 3-0 to us. My Dad was right Eddie Stobarts did bring good luck. My mum came and picked us up and we went to Chorley to stay at a friends house.

Maisie Lee (age 9)

May 2011

Sunday morning and its soon time to leave for Old Trafford ... a quick count up to make sure we haven't lost anyone and we're on our way. The lads look like 'dedicated followers of fashion' in their new blue whistles and the Marie Currie daffs set them off a treat ... even Tommo !

The game for me was the normal mixture of excitement, horror, prayers and trying desperately to act like a grown-up. Those first twenty five minutes in the second-half were 'difficult', but our defence stood tall and true giving Paul plenty of protection and then came the 'Magnificent Seven'.

Seven minutes of football carnage and mayhem that will ensure Rowe, CMS and McCann join the ranks alongside Charlery and Clarke in Posh play-off history, gentlemen, we salute you.

It was overall, a magnificent team performance, each and every one played their heart out and you can't ask for more. Job done … for now.

As the final whistle approached Darragh, Barry and myself wandered down to the dug-out so that we could congratulate the Management Team and the players ... but the next half-hour or so to me was more like a dream sequence from Avatar … graphic colour, incredible noise, strange goings-on and it definitely felt like another planet on that Old Trafford bowling green.

Having had the privilege of being able to join everyone on the pitch, my abiding memory is of the massive heaving wall of delirious Posh supporters wildly cheering and chanting to the lads for our third promotion in four years .... while it was great winning away at Hereford and Colchester to go up automatically, this was different class and how they celebrated.

The singing and support throughout the whole game had been magnificent but the wall of sound as you walked towards the massed ranks of the London Road faithful was truly special. You could see what it meant to all the players and Management Team, the 'dad dancing' started, Charlie drenched anyone who came near him, Litt's wore every hat, flag, t-shirt, wig and scarf that he could get his hands on and Joe & Hibbo did the 'Crouchie Robot' in their shiny new leg braces, oh dear !

As the fans slowly started to depart to join the victorious convoy of coaches, cars, trains and the ET's private helicopter for Adi and Swanny heading back down the A1, the players jigged back to the dressing room and then the hotel for a well deserved evening of needle-point, cake-making and a crazy hand or two of dominos, these boys know how to party !

And ...

Here we go again, the challenge is simple, to be competitive and retain Championship status, the execution will be stretching. We will certainly be better prepared with the experience of our last visit but none of the opposition will roll over to accommodate us. However, let's enjoy the moment ... and the moment was the 81st minute at Stadium MK ...

"Peterborough have been awarded a dubious penalty ... McCann steps up to take it ... 3-2 and Posh are back in it"

Bob Symms

I only went to one Posh game in the 2010/11 season. Old Trafford. Which makes me a fair weather,bandwagon jumping, glory hunter. Only it doesn't. Not really.

You see, I've put in the hours, the miles, the stupid bloody away games at Hartlepool on a Tuesday night, the pointless bloody friendlies at Baldock in July. I've given up valuable drinking time to sell the TPE before games, and given many hours up to help PISA's cause. I've had the season tickets and I've still got the tattoo. Oh yes, and I was 'that 30 year old mascot'. But back in 2006, life changed when my first daughter came along, and in 2008 my second. Whatever Posh had thrown at me over the years, nothing could prepare me for that. You don't get a manual with kids, so it's not really relevant whether they were good or not, but they turned our life upside down to the point that Posh had to come a distant second.

Sure I've been to some games these last few years, ironically more in the Championship in 2009/10 (mainly because there were more midweek games, before the glory hunter thing rears its head again), but work commitments added to the load in 2010/11. And so it was that, by May 29th, the only interaction I'd had with Posh was on the Radio or on Sky. Shoddy, I know. But there it is.

I'm as grateful as the next man that Mr MacAnthony's presence at Posh has given so many memorable days out, and enabled us to grace better stadiums. And I appreciate the fact that the football is a little bit better than the Wile era. But, actually, these things are just a catalyst. For what, you ask? For remembering what being a Poshie is really about. In the week leading up to Old Trafford, I had contact from people I hadn't seen in months or even years. Just for a week, my plans for the day actually competed on a level playing field with Dora the Explorer. On the day I saw people I'd probably last seen at a Posh game. Where and when, God knows. All of us Peterborough people but life moves on and now these same faces came together from Liverpool, from Sheffield, from Reading, and from some two horse town in Wiltshire. I even saw a Poshie from Poland who I went to school with. After the game, I had emails from Spain, from France and from Ireland.

Oh yes. We won. And we won in some style. But, if I'm being honest, I'm not convinced that it mattered *that* much to me. Ok, that's maybe easier to say having won the game. But for me, it's people that matter. Players, managers and chairmen come and go. Poshies, to a lesser or greater degree, stay Poshies forever. And for me, seeing so many of those people again was the real highlight of the day (however bloody good McCann's free kick was!).

I got home at night from Old Trafford and had brought a flag for my youngest daughter. The eldest doesn't seem interested, but the there's a real fighting chance with the youngest. I went in to see her, and she was fast asleep. She woke just enough to say 'we won' and had a huge smile on her face when she saw the flag. Time to pass on what being a Poshie is all about, me thinks.

Ryan Hounsell

I awoke at 6:30 am on the day of the game. I wasn't anxious or nervous about it. They had finished above us in the league and had a long unbeaten run so when I was working out my own excuses for losing on the way home I was fully prepared. This was very different from the nerves of the semi-finals, I can't stand MK Dons and to have lost to them would have been unthinkable.

After our initial plan of a minibus to Old Trafford had fallen through we elected to take the 'licker'; eight of us travelling up together and meeting my brother at the ground. He unfortunately hasn't been able to get to a Posh game for a while but I promised him a good day out if nothing else. When meeting the others in the car park before the game I was surprised that one of our group had decided to paint his face blue. He thought he was showing support but just looked like an overgrown, homosexual smurf. We ensured he didn't forget this throughout the day. Our coach arrived and looked like it would actually manage to get to Old Trafford which was a relief. The coach pulled out of the car park half an hour late and through a large number of Poshies whose coaches hadn't arrived.

The journey to the game was quiet, apart from a near miss with the central barrier just short of Stamford and a bloke who had taken the bizarre decision to go to the game dressed as a duck who was sat in front of us.

On arrival at the ground we met up with my brother. The nerves began to kick in a little and so to calm them a few beers were in order. You know it's going to be a good day when they make mistakes in your favour and we were served with more beer than we had paid for. We walked into the seating area to be greeted with the blue and white blocks of Believe t-shirts but the noise of the Posh fans who had also decided that today was going to be a good day out regardless.

What happened over the next 90 minutes will be reported elsewhere in a much better way than I could hope to write. Although I am willing to lay money that the vast majority knew that McCann was going to score for the third goal; I think that even Benno had a good idea but knew he could do nothing about it. I hugged men I had never met before, my throat ached with singing and supporting and my phone was going beserk with text messages from friends watching the game all over the world.

When we finally got on the bus to go home the journey was relatively subdued. The journey back broken up by more cards, baiting of rather depressed looking fans on Huddersfield coaches, mini sing-songs and reflections of an already great day. The decision was also made to go straight into town on return to celebrate. Our coach driver obviously had the same intention as he drove back to Peterborough with the skill and speed of Lewis Hamilton ensuring we were first back.

So off into town for a few quiet drinks and a chance to relive another great day in the recent history of Posh. On entering one of the pubs in town we discovered a band were on and thinking it a good idea at the time we decided to serenade them with a chorus of "Ee Ei Ee Ei Ee Ei O – Up the football league" we go at the end of each of their songs. After the first line we discovered many in the bar willing to join in with us. Moving on to another bar we discovered they were serving any drink at 90p a go. In the early hours, when my legs were being controlled by someone else I headed back home. After giving the taxi driver a full rendition of Posh songs and I think a rather generous tip.

When people ask football fans why they spend the money, time effort and emotion supporting their team in all kinds of horrific weather, wayward places and dilapidated stadiums the answer is simple. For days like this !

Rhys Thrower

Play off thoughts

My brother had secured us excellent seats in the North Stand. It offered superb views of every moment of play but after Posh had opened the scoring and gone straight on the attack I couldn't figure out why everybody around me was celebrating a corner so wildly. It took me a good five seconds to spot that Craig Mackail-Smith's deflected shot had somehow found its way into the net. I look forward to celebrating more set pieces with wild abandon this coming season.

But one thing I did see from the North Stand was the best builder's arse in football on the young brunette lady who was placing t-shirts underneath the Npower sign which the players gathered behind for their champagne spraying celebrations.

Paul Myland

As the minutes ticked down and we knew we had won, what a strange feeling that was, knowing we had won. Not since 1992, have I seen so many people so happy. People ready to chat to complete strangers, even give them a hug after the goals had flown in. It was a great time to people watch, stood waiting for the final whistle to blow and the euphoria in peoples eyes as we all danced to the victory we had just witnessed. My thoughts quickly turned to my two year-old son, and my hope that he would have brilliant days out like this (as well as the 3-0 defeats at Hartlepool on a Tuesday night) to look forward to.

I was only 15 in 1992, and for me nothing will ever compare to it but that last few minutes of play at Old Trafford will live with my until my dying day.

Jamie Jones, Standingontheglebe.co.uk

May 2011

There probably isn't much that I can add about this game that hasn't been said already, possibly more articulately, by others. What I will say, however, is that I have never felt as proud to be a Posh fan as I do at this moment.

Subsequent teams have a lot to live up to.

Pat McDevitt, Glasgow

I can't say I had much sleep during the week before the final. None of it had anything to do with the actual game but more to do with a 72 seater double-decker luxury coach I had booked for the journey on behalf of PISA 2000.

What with people dropping out, people requesting seats only to then realise a mate or more normally their bloody missus had already booked some other way of getting up there my nerves were all over the place. Eventually after upsetting some members (including incredibly some who didn't even have our coach as an option at any time) we were all done by the Thursday.

There was a couple of chaps I had to let down right at the last minute to a slight cock-up but they were understanding so on the Friday I could at last sit down and relax only for the nerves to kick in once again as I thought about what could or couldn't go wrong. I had a nightmare that the coach didn't turn up. Then after I got to sleep a new nightmare began where 172 passengers turned up instead of the 72!

Lastly after finally getting off for the third time the dream turned into a strange one where the driver was Fry and the conducter was Jim Gannon. I had to get up. It was 5.00. I went on londonroad.net and posted the question whether I was the first up. I wasn't by a long way.

The coach wasn't due till 7 but as we pulled into Grove Street there was the coach but it was disappearing into the distance so my nightmare looked like it was coming true. Turns out the driver was just finding a place to turn round due to the size of the coach. Don't tell the police but we had a good drink once on the road and successfully got rid of any evidence in the services only 30 miles from Manchester. Good job really as later I found out 16 drivers were fined £500 each for allowing the police to find the empties on their respective coaches.

We arrived at The Tollgate around 10.30. A very good drink took place and some meeting up of fellow .netters from all over the country and world

We know how damm good the game was and the result and our journey home was trouble free apart from having to listen to 'udders fans incredibly rewriting history on the Yorkshire based radio stations.

Back at Eb's just in time to watch the highlights of the game. The into town and home by 3.15am, fully 22 hours after I left.

A great day and none of my bad dreams came true. Another great PISA express and hopefully next season in the Championship we will have many more.

Adi Mowles

As the final whistle went at London Road I made an odd, strangulated noise. It started as a screaming celebration but my brain quickly caught up with my voice box and both parties agreed that silence was preferable to waking up a sleeping toddler. You see, foolishly, I elected to watch the 2nd leg of MK Dons at home instead of in the pub. Had I been in the pub, my fellow Leeds based Posh fans would have understand why I was jumping around the place screaming. My wife merely looked at me as if I was a salivating moron.

The next morning I was sat at work, a ridiculous place to be given the circumstances. There was no way on Earth it was going to be possible for me to function, I spent the day on the internet and emailing friends. In a particularly serious moment of hysteria I agreed to purchase eight tickets for Old Trafford. It seemed reasonable at the time, but come the following Monday I realised what a mistake I made. It took two hours and two computers to get eight tickets in a row and three days waiting for the tickets during which my stress levels increased exponentially. My, usually calm, internet persona exploded into a serious of thoughtless (and at times abusive) rants and my home life suffered as my nerves evolved into manic depression. One minute I'd be a wreck, muttering to myself about Royal Mail and gently rocking. The next minute I'd be throwing my two-year old daughter in the air and singing Posh We Are at the top of my voice. By the Saturday she had learnt the words and was singing "na na na na Boro going up" at regular intervals. Rather than amuse me, it sent me further into a spiral of nervous tension

Finally, the longest week in history ended and Sunday appeared. I'd had my usual pre-match dream. The one where I was playing for Posh, but my football skills are still as they are now. Charlie Lee was shouting at me as I failed to control the ball and Mick Halsall gave me a bollocking for missing a sitter. Mick Halsall always plays for Posh in my dreams. I walked the long way to the bus stop, it's a mile out of my way but it takes me over the M62 and I was interested to see if there was a convoy of Posh fans – there wasn't.

Leeds train station appeared to be a meeting place for every Huddersfield fan in the world. Feeling conspicuous in my Posh top I found Mark, Ian, Scott and his kids in Wetherspoons. Dave was running late and would meet us in Manchester, so we departed. We were surprised to get a seat on the train. We were outnumbered 20:1 by Huddersfield fans and this was before the train pulled into Huddersfield station where apparently 2,000 people were queuing outside the ticket hall.

At Manchester we were joined by Diego and made plans to find a pub, wait for Dave, get a tram, find another pub and go to the game. Our plans were thwarted at the first hurdle. Whilst Manchester has an abundance of pubs, finding one to let kids in proved difficult. We eventually found a soulless sports bar near the cinema that sold expensive Guinness in plastic beakers. We'd taken so long to find a pub that Dave turned up whilst we were still buying drinks. After a swift pint we got on a tram, the wrong tram as it turned out. It still dropped us relatively close to Old Trafford, but not near any of the allotted Posh pubs, so we decided to go soak up the atmosphere in and around the ground and drink the warm Singha lager on offer instead

I'm a quiet supporter, I don't chant much, I don't tend to shout, I don't really see why I should have to stand up to prove I love a Football team I've spent £60 to see. That said around the 70 minute mark (I think) Craig Mackail-Smith seemed like he'd broken free of the last man only to be hacked to the ground. It was at this moment that the nerves finally got the better of me. I jumped up screaming at the ref to send the defender off, minutes later I was up again shouting at the ref – demanding a penalty even though I could see Boyd was outside the area and had probably dived anyway. McCann took the free kick, the ball went into the penalty area, hit somebody possibly on their head and suddenly the ball was in the goal. I'm clearly not a sports journalist, but this is exactly how I saw it.

Maybe I could have reflected on it a touch more after the celebrations, which involved Diego jumping at me with his arms outstretched. In the melee I knocked over someones coffee covering their coat with the contents. They didn't seem to mind and as they were drying off the coat I became aware that Craig Mackail-Smith was bearing down on goal, he shot, the ball travelled at a snails pace towards the goal, at least that's how it seemed. It nestled into the corner and I went bezerk, I looked around to give Diego a return hug, but he was embracing Ian – I muscled my way in for a threesome before jumping up the aisle to embrace a random bloke and back down the aisle to hug the guy who's coffee I'd split.

Two goals in what, two minutes? Normally I would have injected myself with a healthy dose of cynicism after a 1-0 lead, this time I hadn't had time. Still 2-0 isn't as concrete as all that. I've seen Posh concede two in 10 minutes before and I was ruling nothing out. That was until McCann scored, my memory may be faulty but as the ball went in the net I'm sure the sky went bright and rays of sunshine broke through the clouds, I felt as if I was having some kind of religious experience. That God was showing his approval at the events on the pitch. I don't even believe in God but for that split second I was a convert. I was one step away wearing Jesus sandals and clapping to Kumbaya. As it was, less than half an hour later I was doing something even less likely than finding Jesus, I was singing Status Quo songs.

I arrived home hoarse. I could only communicate to my wife through a serious of squeaks, but the mere fact I was bouncing around the room was enough for her to gauge my mood. I was still bouncing around Asda the next day, I was still bouncing on Tuesday in work. The following weekend I was bouncing around Leeds Tropical World and today, nine whole days after the match I'm still bouncing...... and I can't get f**king Status Quo out of my head.

Andy Gardner

I am Paul Leadbitter, aka Seoul Posh. Despite the name, I moved from Seoul to Hong Kong a couple of years ago, but haven't bothered to change the name. Before Seoul Posh, I was Bournemouth Posh for obvious reasons and before that KL Posh (I think) when I lived in Kuala Lumpur.

I very rarely get back these days, due to work. In fact, I haven't been back in the footy season since very early in season 2009/10, when I saw the Posh draw 1-1 at QPR. We should have won that day as CMS had a good goal disallowed.

Ever since then, my only contact has been through the internet: I can't imagine what it must have been like for expats supporting the Posh before the www. Either very expensive, making phone calls after/during every match, or very frustrating waiting for the Sunday papers to arrive on Wednesday.

I try to listen to Posh Player for the live games: 10pm for a

3pm kick off and 2.45am for 7.45pm. But the reception and connection is often very bad. I also quite often listen to the opposition commentary when Bob Burrows gets too much for me. I have tried umpteen times to watch the play off final on Posh Player but have still not got as far as kick off before it packs up. I will have to buy the DVD set.

My job involves a lot of travel. I was sitting in an airport in the middle of China during the first leg with MK Dons, and could not get internet access. But I could send emails through Blackberry, so I emailed my daughter in the UK and asked her what the score was. Not nice to be told 3-1 down, when you're sitting in a miserable airport on a miserable Sunday night. But then she emailed again to say 3-2, which made me feel much better.

For the return leg, I just could not stay up, because I had a major meeting the next day. But I woke up with about 10 minutes to go, and just caught the final few minutes on Posh Player. 2-0. Fantastic. Couldn't go back to sleep after that but very nearly did in the major meeting.

For the final, I had sussed out the bar in Hong Kong where I was going to watch it. But on the Friday, I had to agree to go to Mumbai for a meeting on the Monday. The only flight I could get on was Sunday evening so I was literally up in the air throughout the whole final. As soon as we landed I was on the Blackberry to my daughter. 3-0 she said. I asked her to promise she wasn't joking. No, she said: Posh scored three times in seven minutes. Still not convinced, I asked her who scored (she has no interest in Posh and wouldn't know any names). She immediately came back with Rowe, Mackail-Smith and McCann so I got off the plane with a huge smile on my face, and spent half the night in the hotel online, reading all about it.

Paul Leadbitter, Hong Kong

So my partner was about to start her new job when late on the Sunday night before we decided that as we have no holidays booked as yet best think about it so she can tell her new employers that we have already booked vacation. We went online, found a nice looking place in Lanzarote. We had a quick think about it then booked it, agreed that she should tell her new bosses that she was away for a week at the end of May and again in the week of the beer festival.... job done.

Then the play offs come around. I look online to check the dates and discover to my horror that we are due to leave on the Thursday before the final. F*ck, f*ck, f*ckerty f*ck... were among the expletives I let out as I prowled around the room feeling so angry with my gross stupidity.

Online again. Flight, Monarch airlines from Lanzarote to Manchester, Sat 28th May at 8.40, brilliant! and only 47 Euros. Return flight Monday at 4pm from Manchester arriving back in Lanzarote at 8.30 in the evening or get to Heathrow and catch Iberia airlines flight to Madrid and link to Lanzarote arriving back at 1.30pm. All details scribbled on paper

She accepts the idea, maybe begrudgingly at first but in principle all seems sorted. Now, for the small issue of getting to the final. All I really want is a 0-4 victory at the building site MK, then I can book the flights about. MK away, as usual my team made it difficult for me. Losing 3-2 gives me two choices. Book flight and maybe throw £150 to the wind or wait until after the second leg, which I opt to do.

Brilliant night at London Road, straight home to watch the recording, brilliant viewing I am on such a high. Tip toe up to bed so as not to wake her. To be greeted with the question: " Did we win? I nodded. "So I will have a couple of nights in Lanzarote on my own then". My god she still loves me, well she did until I made her get up and watch the semi with me (*oooerrrr; Editor*).

On our flight to Lanzarote everything is packed as normal. T shirts, shorts, sun cream, Posh flag and wet weather gear. Her ladyship manages to inform everybody she talks to that she will be alone for two nights while I swan off. Several tell her that the Spanish waiters may be available. I don't care a jot. She can do what she wants as long as we win.

Flight back to Manchester, delayed for three hours. Watch Champions league final with a plane full of Mancunians. Arrive Manchester 03:15 drizzling. What shall I do? Walk to the ground or hang around in the multi storey car park until morning? Me my flag my duty free fags and Match ticket. Balls to that book myself in a hotel.

Taxi to the ground at noon. Call Damo to find out where he is parked. We meet up and make our way to the turnstiles. Pissed wet through, wet weather gear was a brilliant idea. Swamped by noisy bastard Tykes. Are there any other sort?

Into to the stadium, concourse throbbing with Posh fans, this is more like it. Brilliant performance. Still throwing Nilesh up in the air, celebrating the first goal, when the second went in. Impressed with our defence for only the third time this season. Still a little twitchy until McCanns brilliant third. Noisy bastard Tykes all go quiet. Final whistle mad celebration all round until I realise that I have seen CMS for the last time in a Posh shirt so it was tinged with a little sadness.

Back to Heathrow. Great flights to Madrid and then onto Lanzarote. Her ladyship meets me from the taxi. Tells me how she had everyone watching in the bar cheering for the mighty Posh, good girl. Back on my sun bed at 2.30pm. Best holiday I have ever had.

Steve Collison

My Old Trafford build up started on the Friday when a client, a Huddersfield fan, came in for his hair cut. We were both as nervous about the game as each other, whilst the snipping of hair was taking shape there was an in depth analysis taking place of our respective teams previous encounters and recent performances. One thing that we both agreed on that it was it was right that the Imposters hadn't got through as they don't deserve their place in the league.

Sunday saw us getting up and leaving the house at 8.30. Half an hour behind schedule mainly due to Steve deciding what to put on his feet to protect his blistered toes after his little stroll around London. We picked up Ashley's mate Joe - who thought we had forgotten him - en route. The journey was going well until we hit the hills - my car does not do hills - with foot flat on the pedal we still only just nudged 60mph but after about 3 hours we saw the sight of Old Trafford.

Bedecked with flag and scarfs we made our way to the ground defiantly outnumbered by the Huddersfield fans who were very vocal and cocky about their chances of beating us. After meeting up with people and chatting outside we made our way in and found our seats as the tension and excitement built up. The teams came out lead by the one and only Fergie - well the one that matters to us Posh fans.

As the game kicked off I don't really remember too much about the first-half except those two near misses by CMS and before we knew it was half time. Second-half and we were shooting towards our end, despite that few 15-20 mins that 'uddersfield' put a bit of pressure on it was us playing the football then Boyd's foul 15,000 + were praying for the penalty convinced it was inside the box, but what did it matter when McCann stepped up there was that hope ....this is going to be 1-0. Who scored it didn't matter at the time as the noise was incredible having only just been sat down again after celebrating with Steve and Ashley no sooner were we all screaming and celebrating like girls again with that CMS goal ...goal No 99.

Then McCann steps up again for the free kick......the look on Steve's face was 'have we really just scored three goals in seven mins'. What an amazing day and season to be a Posh fan and to celebrate a play-off final win with Ashley was great as I wiped a tear away and there was a few in Steve's eyes too as the final whistle went. Making our way out and celebrating with people we knew it was all about that amazing seven minutes of football.

I'm glad that I won't be having anymore children as I'm sure their middle names would be Gabby, Ryan, Charlie, Craig, George, Lee, Grant, Joe, James, Mark, Paul, Tommy, Chris, and for good measure Darragh and Darren.

As for that Huddersfield fan well he phoned on Tuesday morning and congratulated me on our win and said that the better team had won and the difference had been CMS and McCann and that spell of seven minutes of football.

Thank-you Posh for making a great exciting season an amazing one with so many highlights and making the Thorpe household an extremely happy one too.

Jo Thorpe

It was a long wait for the Final at Old Trafford. I was envious of everybody who was able to go. I was reading the posts about the number of tickets sold and how it should have been more.

How I would have loved to be able to go to Manchester to see that game. But I knew it was being shown on the television here and I was happy to stay up until midnight that day and sit in my rumpus room, on my own, waiting for the start of the most important game of the season. I'd restricted myself to only a few beers because I didn't want to fall asleep and miss any of this game.

I logged into LondonRoad.net and clicked on to the match thread. Of course it was quiet. Everybody was at the match. But a few overseas and other fans were watching the TV and watching the match thread as well.It is hard to describe how tense it all was.

At half time, when it was 0-0, posh.netters - CanadaPosh, Italian Posh and me - were worried sick that we might not win this game. But at about 1:45 am we scored and what a goal it was. I was running around the house like a mad thing. I quickly settled in front of the TV again, worrying once more that Huddersfield would find the back of the net. But within a space of seven minutes we were 3-0 up.

That last goal by McCann was brilliant. As I posted to the match thread on LondonRoad.net " 3-0 !!! I can't believe it. That was as good as a Beckham goal."

Soon after, CanadaPOSH posted " We are going up say we are going up" And how right he was. It was about 2 am when the final whistle was blown and I had another beer to celebrate the fact that the Posh were now in the Championship.

I then ran outside shouting and cheering and disturbed a couple of possums enjoying the what they thought was a quiet night. But it is cold here at this time of the year and I was soon back inside again,

What a great night it was.

Tony Pell

An inspired and brave choice five months earlier by Darragh to bring back Darren Ferguson to the club re -ignited the spark and whilst automatic promotion was missed the Posh made sure we were in the lottery that is the play offs. After showing the MK Dons the door we were on our way to Old Trafford. Could we make it a hat trick of play-off wins?

If anyone thought the play-off games against MK Dons were emotional it was about to get worse as Posh fans began to plan their away day and wrestle with Ticketmaster for match day tickets. With 30,000 tickets available there was never going to be a problem getting to see the match, however as the game grew closer and tickets had not been received many, including me, began to foam around the mouth and question Ticketmaster's outrageous admin and postage costs.

Manchester is a bit of a way from Devon so it was clear that if we were to enjoy the day to the full we needed to call in a favour or two. A quick call to an ex army pal living in Bury and accommodation was sorted. Saturday morning and our adventure begins as we leave our sleepy Devon village for the bright lights of Manchester. The journey up was slow but who cares we were off to see the boys in blue play at Old Trafford. Arriving in Bury late afternoon, we cracked open the beers and settled down for the rest of the day to enjoy great company and watch some minor Champions league match.

Woke up Sunday morning to an overcast sky and rain – yep we were up north. It was going to be a long day so after a good fry up the three of us set off at 11am. First stop the Tollgate pub. Arrived to find the place already full of Poshies - some nervous, some excited and some already showing signs of having had a few lemonades. With just over 90 mins to kick off we decided to make our way to the ground planning to call in at a few pubs along the way. Wrong decision – 50 yards down the road and the heavens opened – yep it always rains in Manchester. Turn left and into the closest hostelry to dry off and once the weather had changed from monsoon to drizzle we set off again. Time for one last beer and a nervous piss. Find our seats and soak up the atmosphere. What an atmosphere and spectacle it was....Udders 30,000 fans looked good at the Stretford End and the blue and white Believe T shirts looked impressive – but it was the 15,000 Poshies who were making the noise. Enter the teams to a massive roar from both sets of fans – this was it. The national anthem brought a lump to the throat.

Fortunately we were at the back of block E237 and to a man, woman and child everyone was standing, chanting, clapping as the ref blew the whistle and we were off. God we sounded so loud – we wanted this, we deserved this so come on lads do it for us. Lee Clark the 'Udders manager had for some reason chosen to play one up front and pack the midfield in an attempt to nullify the influence of Grant McCann. He was obviously frightened of our attacking threat. Although Posh were dominating we were unable to take advantage and Udders began to settle and pose a threat themselves.

Forty five minutes gone, we were satisfied. Posh were clearly the better footballing side. For all their fans Udders had also lost the first half singing competition and as the strong sunshine beat back the rain clouds – surely this was our day. Time for another beer.

We thought it would happen and it did. Huddersfield came out strongly and began to force the game and for the first time their fans began to make some real noise. The Posh defence so often criticised was being tested – this was Huddersfield giving it their all. Zak and Bennett held firm. A break on the Huddersfield right saw Bassey skinned and as their player broke into the box he fired a shot in from an acute angle...off it went from the crossbar and although we did not know at the time Jones had managed to get a finger to it. For all their hard work and possession they could not break us down and that was their best effort of the game.

The game was entering the last phase but we had weathered all that the Terriers could throw at us now it was our time...our moment. Posh fans grew louder as we once again began to push forward. A good skilful move saw Boyd floored as he danced into the area....cue 15,000 Poshies shouting penalty but the ref had other ideas. Free kick just outside the box. Another wave of noise from the faithful. Come on Posh just put one away for us. Up steps McCann to drive in the ball into the six yard area and from the mass of defenders little Tommy Rowe glances in the header and the net bulged. The release of emotion was fantastic. Beginning to well up a little now. Posh were now tenacious and an interception by set Boyd on his way down the left... a few step overs and then he pulled the ball back inside the 18 yard box to CMS. Almost in slow motion CMS shoots and after a deflection the ball rolls into the corner of the net. If we thought the wave of emotion after the first goal was something, this was even better...absolutely mental.

Huddersfield were deflated and it showed, frustration

creeping in they became more desperate up front and they began to open up at the back. A ball forward to CMS who just runs and runs – a defenders nightmare and inevitably he was pushed to the ground. Another free kick in a similar position to the first. Captain Marvel McCann steps up again, the ball lifts up and over the wall to nestle in the top corner.

Better than Beckham, game over. With tears in our eyes and man hugs all round we could really, really party now.

If you cannot go up as champions this has to be the best way to do it...what a day, what a match and what a fantastic team and fans.

John Middleton

Darren Ferguson; the greatest comeback since Lazarus

Paul Mitchell